Working the Land

Working

the Land

The Stories of Ranch and Farm Women in the Modern American West

SANDRA K. SCHACKEL

 University Press of Kansas

Published by the University Press of Kansas (Lawrence, Kansas
66045), which was organized by the Kansas Board of Regents
and is operated and funded by Emporia State University,
Fort Hays State University, Kansas State University, Pittsburg
State University, the University of Kansas, and Wichita State
University

Library of Congress Cataloging-in-Publication Data

Schackel, Sandra.
  Working the land : the stories of ranch and farm women in
the modern American West / Sandra K. Schackel.
      p.   cm.
  Includes bibliographical references and index.
  ISBN 978-0-7006-1780-7 (cloth : alk. paper) 1. Women
ranchers—West (U.S.)—History—20th century.
2. Women farmers—West (U.S.)—History—20th century.
3. Women ranchers—West (U.S.)—Interviews. 4. Women
farmers—West (U.S.)—Interviews. 5. Ranch life—West
(U.S.)—History—20th century. 6. Farm life—West (U.S.)—
History—20th century. 7. West (U.S.)—Social life and
customs—20th century. 8. West (U.S.)—Social conditions—
20th century. 9. Interviews—West (U.S.) 10. Oral history—
West (U.S.) I. Title.
  F596.S34 2011
  978'.033—dc22
                                             2011007962

British Library Cataloguing-in-Publication Data is available.

Printed in the United States of America

10 9 8 7 6 5 4 3 2 1

The paper used in this publication is recycled and contains
30 percent postconsumer waste. It is acid free and meets the
minimum requirements of the American National Standard for
Permanence of Paper for Printed Library Materials Z39.48-1992.

Contents

Illustrations

Preface

My home is the vast, open landscape of south-central Idaho, at once a
sanctuary, a source of strength, and a heartache.
—Diane Josephy Peavey, *Bitterbrush Country*

Not many ranch or farm folks would disagree with Idaho author Diane
Josephy Peavey. Most would likely acknowledge her poignant expression
of both beauty and disappointment in their shared lifestyle. From the
"big sky" over Montana's cattle pastures to the irrigated fields flanking
Idaho's Snake River to sagebrush-covered mesas in New Mexico, those
who live on western farms and ranches today share mixed feelings about
their way of life. Most of the women I interviewed for this book praised
the benefits of raising children along with cows and harvesting potatoes
or pinto beans; it is the way in which agriculture in this country has
shifted over the last fifty years that causes the heartache. As family farms
slowly disappear from the western landscape to make way for larger,
more efficient methods of raising crops and animals, or to make way
for growing subdivisions instead of crops, a certain nostalgia is settling
over lost homesteads and cattle ranches. In the 1970s, when agribusiness
began to bear down on small operations and farmers and ranchers were
told to "Get big or get out," many families had to make a tough choice.
Some sold out and moved to town or to warmer, easier climes; others
took out loans, bought up more land and even larger equipment, and
stayed in the business. But many other farmers and ranchers have hung
on for a variety of reasons, not the least of which is that they love their
lives lived close to the land.

My father was not one of those types; hence I do not have a firsthand
agricultural background. I grew up in a small rural agricultural community in east central Illinois, but I was a "town kid." My memories of
farm life come from the few days each summer that my younger brother

and sister and I spent on my aunt and uncle's seed-corn farm twenty minutes north of town. We loved those visits with my dad's sister and her husband and our cousins. This was the last farm still in the family, and my aunt and uncle stayed on the land long enough to be recognized as an Illinois Centennial Farm in 1972.[1] My dad was the only son among three sisters, all born on "the farm place" south of town. As a boy, he quickly tired of the agricultural lifestyle, but he stayed on the farm for two years past high school graduation. Then in 1938, the Chicago & Eastern Illinois Railroad built a roundhouse in Villa Grove and began to hire local men. Dad fudged his age by a year (the minimum was 21) and signed on, grateful for a regular paycheck and "lighter" workload. He married, raised three children, and retired from the railroad after forty-three years, never regretting having left the farm.

While I grew up surrounded by soybean and corn fields—and the regular whistle of trains passing through town—I didn't really experience what the farm kids had to do every day. When I visited the family farm, I knew Uncle Wilbur went out (early!) on his tractor every morning and Aunt Lois cooked for the family in a small kitchen with only cold running water. Then the five of us would run off to play in the haymow—my hay fever was soon out of control—chase the pigs, ride the newfangled riding mower, or watch with fascination as our cousins milked the family's two cows. What could be hard about this kind of lifestyle? On the other hand, I did not even consider marrying a local farmer and becoming a farmwife, as some of my girlfriends did. Like many teens in postwar America, I wanted to leave the small-town life for college, then "create a life" of my own choosing. It was quite a while before I actually met that goal, but I did marry, have two babies quickly and a third one a few years later, and help my husband through dental school. We left our small rural community in 1961 and never looked back, or so it seemed. In reality, we did return home for visits and reunions, and over time, I came to realize that this agricultural landscape in the heart of middle America had become part of my identity. I didn't realize how much until the idea for this book arose in the mid-1990s.

By this time, the new genre of western women's history was about fifteen years old and growing rapidly. One day agricultural historian R. Douglas Hurt, then at Iowa State University, called to invite me to write a chapter for a book he was putting together on the rural West since World

War II.[2] In particular, he wanted a chapter on rural women's experiences. When I discovered a lack of research material on the subject, I saw an opportunity to use one of my favorite research methods, the oral history interview, to record agricultural women's stories. Basically, I wanted to know how their lives, or their mothers' or grandmothers' lives, on the farm or ranch had changed in the second half of the twentieth century. My initial intentions turned out to be overly ambitious: to interview women across the American West, which, by most accounts, would include seventeen states, more than a daunting task for one in her middle age(s). In my next proposal, I substantially reduced that number to half a dozen or so. I began in the two states I know best, Idaho and New Mexico, and extended my range beyond their borders to west Texas, southern and eastern Arizona, southern Colorado, and eastern Oregon.

Eschewing the formal requirements of a quantitative study, I found my subjects via the "snowball method"; that is, one woman led me to another, who told me to talk to her neighbor, who said, "You should also interview my mother-in-law on the next ranch," and so on. The result is nearly fifty interviews with women ranging in age, at the time of the interview, from 24 to 83; some of them retired, some working only in the farmhouse, others driving tractors and running cattle, and many working in town at wage-earning jobs so the family could afford to stay on the farm. My subjects include Mexican/Hispanic Americans, Basques, Japanese Americans, and women of Euro-American heritage; sometimes their husbands came in for lunch and spoke their thoughts into the tape recorder on the kitchen table as well. They are single, married, widowed, with and without children, working- and middle-class. Two women in New Mexico have ranched together since the 1960s; several have outlived husbands and do the work themselves; one woman wrapped meat in the family slaughterhouse weekly in addition to farming; two others gave piano lessons to provide additional income; a woman in Arizona works her family's three-generation cattle ranch while her husband works as a stonemason in nearby Benson; a former 1960s activist has taken up environmental farming while continuing to plant pinto beans on her Hispanic family's 40 acres in southern Colorado. Multicultural and multigenerational, these voices represent a small sample of women living in the rural West in the late twentieth century.

Armed with a list of prospective interviewees, I sent a letter describing my project, then followed up with a phone call to see if they were interested in talking to me. More than one woman responded by saying, "Oh, I haven't done anything unusual; I've just been a farmwife all my life," implying her life was not important enough to document. Others were ready for me when I arrived to do the interview and had made notes ahead of time of experiences they wanted to share. I developed a questionnaire (included in the appendix) but basically used it to keep myself on track during the interview. I did send it ahead to a few women with mixed results; one woman lost it, another forgot to look it over, and one woman had the questionnaire in hand when I arrived and proceeded to answer the questions in such a rapid-fire way that the interview was over in no time! Only one woman turned down my request, pleading shyness; the more common response, as mentioned above, was to provide me with more names of people I should interview. Overall, my subjects seemed pleased that someone was interested in the everyday details of their lives and were more than willing to share their experiences with me.

As I listened to and transcribed the tapes over the past decade plus, I found several themes or currents running through the women's words. These themes provide the structure for the book and comprise the five chapter topics. The topics include the satisfaction found in the farming/ranching lifestyle; the flexibility of gender roles; off-farm wage work; farms and ranches as sites for tourist recreation; and agricultural activism. Some of the interviewees spoke to all these themes, while others talked of just two or three. Neither my survey nor this book attempts to cover the myriad of issues that comprise the agricultural sector in our country today. My original intention, to examine how an agricultural woman's life changed in the second half of the twentieth century, meant that this book would likely not be about agricultural policy (although that topic does arise in chapter 5, on activism), scientific methods of farming, soil composition and climate, or numerous other sundry and related topics. I wanted to hear the women's explanations of why they preferred working in the fields to working in the farmhouse, or not; why they taught school or worked at the bank while living a rural lifestyle; how technology had, or had not, made their lives easier; how they felt when none of their children wanted to inherit the family operation; in general, like a good social historian, I wanted to know about their lives from "the bottom up."

In the following pages, you will meet the women who welcomed me into their homes, shared coffee or iced tea and often a meal, and generally made me glad I had undertaken this project. They became my friends, albeit for a brief moment in time, and all invited me back to talk some more. They were candid about the patriarchal nature of agriculture, frustrated by the public's seeming lack of interest in how food gets to America's kitchen tables, clever in finding ways to supplement farm income, and saddened by disappearing family farms. I was impressed with the ability of these families to adopt, adapt, resist, or make changes in order to retain their way of life. In the epilogue, I have tried to contact as many of the original interviewees as possible in order to bring their life stories into the twenty-first century. Several have died, some have retired and moved to town, while others continue to live and work on the land they love.

Acknowledgments

This book has been in the making since 1995, when I began to think about rural women's lives for a chapter in an anthology on the rural West. R. Douglas Hurt, editor of the resultant volume, *The Rural West since World War II*, gave me free rein to approach the topic however I chose. I had grown up in a small rural town in Illinois, surrounded by fields of corn and soybeans, so I assumed rural women meant farm women. Some of my school classmates took the bus from their farm homes, but the rest of us were "town kids," even though that town boasted a population of just 2,200 in the 1950s.

Because of this narrow small-town view, I approached the assignment assuming I would be gathering materials about twentieth-century western farm women, not small-town women who worked for small wages in town, another dimension of rural women's lives but not one I address here. My focus became farming and ranching women, but when I couldn't find much to build a chapter on, I decided this might be a topic for a book. And since there were few, if any, publications on western farm women, why not go to the source? Armed with a tape recorder and notebook, I began to seek out the voices chronicled here. Thank you, Doug, for setting me on the path to this book.

In the fifteen years that have passed since then, I have gathered a long list of names of farm and ranch women who were willing to spend a few hours with me, telling me their stories. Many of them insisted they "had nothing important to talk about" but kept talking anyway and let me be the judge of their words. I hope I have done them justice. They were welcoming, gracious hosts to a stranger who wanted them to open up about their past lives as well as the present and the changes they experienced along the way. After the coffee and pie or lunch with husbands sitting in, I reluctantly gathered up my equipment and notes and we said our goodbyes. But I carry each and every one of them in my heart, as well as my files, and feel infinitely blessed by their friendship. Thank you, all of you.

During this same period, my life as a professor, teacher, author, and colleague in the Boise State University Department of History continued. I published a second book, an anthology of classroom essays on twentieth-century western women, was promoted to full professor, and continued recording interviews. One of the best and most helpful exercises in compiling the stories here came in the opportunity to present my work at academic conferences over the past decade. These essays became the foundation for the five chapters of the book. For the time and the travel funds, I am very grateful to the university for granting me several College of Social Science and Public Affairs travel grants. I also thank the university for granting me a leave of absence that allowed me time to write as well as collect interviews in west Texas. Colleague and friend Nick Miller has supported and encouraged my work throughout his tenure as department chair. And to Guen Johnson, Department of History Administrative Assistant, many, many thanks for help with all my "last minute" deadlines, rewrites, the copying, and the general nurturing of my professional and personal spirit during this odyssey.

To all the women who provided more names for me to interview—a neighbor, a mother-in-law, or a ranching friend, I say thank you many times over. I have a file box full of names yet to contact. Although I have recorded more than fifty interviews, I was not able to include all the voices in this volume. Perhaps they will be impetus for volume two!

Finally, I thank the University Press of Kansas editors for their patience in allowing me time to picture and frame and write these stories, from Nancy Scott Jackson, who solicited my work at the first conference at which I read one of the chapters, to Ranjit Arab, who has firmly but gently guided my progress in this past year, and Larisa Martin, who has patiently shepherded the book through production. Thank you all for continuing to believe in the work despite the extended "season" of germination, cultivation, and now, finally, the harvest—the many stories of farm and ranch women working the land they love.

Acronyms/Abbreviations

DRA	Dakota Rural Action (South Dakota)
DRC	Dakota Resource Council (North Dakota)
IRC	Idaho Rural Council
LMA	Livestock Marketing Association
NAFTA	North American Free Trade Agreement
NCA	National Cattlemen's Association
NPRC	Northern Plains Resource Council (Montana)
ORA	Oregon Rural Action (Eastern Oregon)
PRBRC	Powder River Basin Resource Council (Wyoming)
R-CALF	Ranchers' and Cattlemen's Action Legal Fund
WCC	Western Colorado Congress (Southwest Colorado)
WORC	Western Organization of Resource Councils

1

"I'd Rather Be on the Farm"
Attitudes toward Ranch and Farmwork

Helen Tiegs knew she wanted to be a farmwife, but those early years on the farm were challenging and sometimes made for a good laugh and good family lore.[1] When I interviewed her the first time in 1995, one of the first things she told me was how she

> pulled some real boo-boos when I was first married. We had a bunch of little chickens in the house in a little pen. They were just new chicks. I didn't know a thing about farming; I didn't know a thing about farm animals or anything else because I was a city girl and . . . he [her husband Don] put some little pheasant eggs in there. And I called my mother-in-law and told her, I said, "These little chickens laid eggs already!" I never lived that down, I'll tell you, I never lived that down.

Nor did she enjoy driving a tractor—"I have but it's been a disaster!" Tiegs quickly learned about farm life, however, and now, over fifty years later, considers herself an important contributor to the success of their family crop farm in Nampa, Idaho, a rapidly growing city 10 miles west of Boise. Referring to herself as the "hub of the wheel," today Tiegs "keeps things going" with the aid of her cell phone. Her role on the family farm has changed little in the years since this city girl married a local farm boy in 1948. Tiegs had not grown up around agriculture, nor did her husband want her to work in the fields. As a result, Tiegs lived the traditional domestic lifestyle expected of middle-class American women in the mid-twentieth century. That is, she was responsible for domestic tasks, which

1

included the care and feeding of a large garden as well as the care and feeding of their children. Like my other informants, Tiegs spoke enthusiastically of her satisfaction with farming as a way of life, saying, "Oh, I love it out here!" In one voice, they told me that a life spent in agriculture means a life lived close to the land, one that is not only challenging on many levels but deeply satisfying as well. "It was all I knew, and I loved it from the start," Martha Ascuena of Mountain Home, Idaho, told me.[2] Carol Inouye of Parma, near Idaho's western border with Oregon, echoed Ascuena's sentiments: "We had a very, very good life and lifestyle."[3]

In *Between Grass and Sky: Where I Live and Work,* Linda M. Hasselstrom self-identifies as a woman, a rancher, and a lover of prairies. As a child on a South Dakota ranch, she carried a little notebook in her pocket in which she noted interesting things about her environment: "how an antelope stamped his feet and whistled when my father and I rode by on our horses; how a meadowlark dragged her wing and whimpered when we got near her nest."[4] In the evening, she wrote her observations in a journal, along with the work she did on the ranch that day. To Hasselstrom, also categorized as a "nature writer," her work and her writing are intertwined; nature to her is both office and home. For the women I interviewed, being in nature was part and parcel of their love for the land. They spoke of never-ending chores, of hailstorms, of animal deaths, of pastel sunrises much in the same way Hasselstrom and others detail "the hard work and challenges posed by a nature that is both destructive and regenerative."[5]

In *Windbreak: A Woman Rancher on the Northern Plains,* Hasselstrom wrote in journal form of a year of her life with her husband on her parents' ranch. In the preface, she describes ranch work this way: "Ranch work, like most jobs, has its routines, its repetition. Our drama comes with the cycles of nature; with the endless absorption with birth and death; with the lives of our neighbors and friends; with the weather, which is a character in the story of our lives."[6]

In her entry for February 11, Hasselstrom speaks to the rapid pace of contemporary life on ranches and farms where neighbors don't often see one another, don't visit on Sundays as they used to or engage as often in community activities:

> To me, this seems as great a danger to the "family farm" . . . this loss of the sense of community, of belonging, of knowing your neighbors.

Ascuena family ranchland east of Mountain Home, Idaho, early 1950s. Courtesy of Martha Ascuena.

It has its drawbacks. I really don't want my neighbors, however sympathetic, to know all my business as they did in the days of the party line telephone, but it would be almost worth it to feel the support, which seems to have vanished.[7]

Hasselstrom reflects the uneasiness felt in farm and ranch families who know their numbers are in decline. The term itself, "family farm," is often romanticized, viewed through the eyes of disenchanted urban dwellers. But agricultural families do not see their way of life as a sentimental form of economic production. Their intention to pass it on is a primary goal, and women are central to this process, passing on their skills, knowledge, and values as well as the farm itself.

None of the women I spoke with denied or ignored the hardships of living on ranches and farms in the last half of the twentieth century, a period of tumultuous and historic changes that altered the shape of American agriculture forever. Nor did they appear to romanticize their lives. Instead, they reiterated their satisfaction with this lifestyle and expressed regrets that it appears to be in decline. In fact, for the last three decades agriculture experts have predicted the demise of the family farm, the last piece of the grand agrarian dream that shaped this country nearly four hundred years ago. The notion that small-to-medium-sized farms are indispensable to American democracy is part of the heritage of Jeffersonian agrarianism.[8] And while the number of small, part-time farms has increased, the total number of farms in the United States has been dropping since the 1930s.

At the turn of the twentieth century, nearly half of all Americans lived on farms. This figure dropped to 30 percent in 1920, declined to less than 3 percent in the 1990s, and fell under 2 percent in the 2000 census.[9] For all kinds of social and economic reasons, small family farms have given way to very large operations frequently referred to as agribusinesses. In 1935, there were 6.8 million farms, averaging 155 acres. In 1960, there were just under 4 million, and by 1982, the figure had dropped to 2.4 million farms while farm size had grown to an average of 433 acres.[10] The trend in the last half century has been an increase in the very large and large family farms while medium and small family farms and rural residences have declined. As a result, farming has become more productive, concentrated, centralized, and dependent on hired rather than family labor, with farms associated with agribusiness accounting for increased farm production.[11] Still, it is not likely that the family farm will disappear from view entirely despite the "farm crisis" that persisted for much of the twentieth century and that accelerated after World War II. Indeed, farmwife Elizabeth Lloyd responded to my query about the farm crisis by commenting that being raised on a farm meant "it was always a crisis, all my life." Farm wives have a great deal to say about weathering the storms that threaten family farms.

During this same period, gender roles in America shifted notably. In the aftermath of World War II, men's and women's roles appeared firmly established, at least for most white middle-class women. As the war came to a close, the Labor Department urged women to lay down their riveting guns and welding torches to return to their sewing machines and ironing boards, not to mention the kitchen and the bedroom, where they would produce both biscuits and babies. Men returning from the front lines needed jobs; women were expected to support their men by returning to the domestic front. Initially, many women responded to this governmental and social directive, and the percentage of women working outside the home fell from 36 percent at the end of the war to 28 percent by 1947. By the end of the decade, however, women were again entering the labor force, albeit in traditionally low-paying, low-skilled "pink-collar" jobs—clerical, sales, and service work—that reinforced sex segregation in the workplace.[12]

Several factors altered the face of both the labor market and consumer habits in the immediate postwar years. Unlike the young working women of earlier eras, the post–World War II female workers were predominantly older, married, middle-class women. And they chose to work for reasons other than patriotism and economic support of the nation during war or depression. Historian William Chafe points out that women went back to work not for "pin money" but because postwar inflation justified, even required, a second income. Rising inflation, along with rising expectations for consumer goods, combined to justify women's return to the workplace.[13] By the 1950s, the rapid growth of consumer culture symbolized by (among other things) the three-bedroom, two-bathroom suburban home, television sets, automobiles with large fins, the home freezer, and packaged cake mixes had triggered a reconstruction of gender roles that played out in the counterculture of the 1960s, the women's movement of the 1970s, and the backlash of the 1980s and 1990s.

Not a group to readily call themselves feminists, ranch and farm women were not immune to gender-shifting patterns within the larger culture. Self-identifying as farmers, ranchers, farmwives, farmhands, even the casual but meaningful term "go-fer," my informants are clear about their roles on family farms and ranches.[14] Their lives had meaning and purpose, and they knew what was expected of them on a daily basis. These women drove tractors, moved irrigation pipe, ordered fertilizer, and often worked in town. Although they frequently carried out traditionally male tasks, many continued to define themselves primarily as farm or ranchwives rather than farmers or ranchers. Tiegs, as noted above, referred to herself as the "hub of the wheel," yet she acknowledges that she has "always kept house" and still spends hours canning fresh fruits and vegetables from her summer garden, saying, "I can't stand to buy a can of tomatoes or peaches." Although she is a traditional farmwife in many ways, Tiegs's roles cross gender boundaries when, for example, she is called away from domestic tasks to go to town for a crucial piece of equipment needed to keep production flowing that day. In this way, her labor, along with her husband's, is central to the overall success of the farming operation.

The Tiegs family farm lies in the heart of Idaho's Treasure Valley just a few miles distant from the bustling capital city of Boise. In the nineteenth century, Boise City (as it was called then) served as a supply center for the gold and silver mining activity that began in the 1860s. With the passage of two federal irrigation measures, the Carey Act in 1894 and the Newlands Reclamation Act in 1902, improved irrigation techniques (and federal funds) soon turned the desert scrubland into verdant fields and farms.[15] As more settlers moved into the valley, dairy farms and cattle ranches began to share this newly irrigated land with fruit orchards and fields of alfalfa, sugar beets, wheat, potatoes, peas, and mint, drawing on the nearby Snake and Boise Rivers as their water source.

As in several other western states prior to World War II, Idaho's population barely numbered one-half million people by 1940. Boise remained a small urban area within the larger rural valley. From a population of 26,130 in 1940, the capital city grew to 102,160 in 1980, while the valley remained heavily agricultural.[16] In the last three decades of the twentieth century, however, rapid urban growth triggered a significant change in the region's economic base as farmland gave way to subdivisions. According to the 2000 census, more than 185,000 people called Boise home, nearly 400,000 in the larger Treasure Valley. Much of this population growth was a result of the city's efforts to draw light industry to the region in the previous thirty years. Home-grown and home-based Micron Technology, world-leading producer of computer chips, led the way in creating well-paying white-collar jobs in the valley. By the turn of the twenty-first century, the city was also home to several corporate headquarters, including Hewlett-Packard's printer division, the Albertsons supermarket chain, Washington Group International (formerly the engineering firm Morrison Knudsen), Boise Cascade, and numerous smaller firms engaged in high-tech production.[17] The resulting influx of employees and their families triggered a shift in land use as the combine and cultivator gave way to the backhoe and Bobcat, marking out subdivisions on the once fertile and still valuable farmland. And, as other farm families across the nation have found, when the land becomes more valuable for growing houses than for growing crops, farm owners are hard-pressed not to sell the family farm to developers.

Transitions in land use such as this are not new. With new, bigger, and more sophisticated farm equipment, increasing crop yields, automated dairy farms, and ever-increasing debt, ranch and farm families have had to explore every possible avenue to maintain their livelihood since WWII. While some families have decided to sell their property to developers or agribusinesses, others struggle in the face of far-reaching transformations because ranching or farming has long been a way of life for them and has brought considerable satisfaction. Martha Ascuena described this lifestyle and her role in it this way: "I always thought I would be a farmer's wife. . . . That's just all I ever wanted to do."

Martha was born in Nebraska in 1921, and her family moved to Idaho in 1926 on the advice and enthusiasm of her dad's brother and family in Nampa, who "kept talking about this wonderful Idaho. . . . He [her dad] hired, I guess you would say, a boxcar and put all our personal things in a boxcar and shipped them out. And then the three families came out in automobiles. And that's how we got here."

While her father leased farmland in the Nampa area, Martha attended local schools and graduated from Nampa High School in 1939. The following year, at age 19, she married Jack Chipman, then gave birth to two sons within the next five years. The newlyweds worked on several farms in southwest Idaho during this period, finally purchasing property west of Boise in 1945, just north of Eagle, currently one of Idaho's fastest growing communities, "where all the big, beautiful homes are now." After seven years on the rich farmland there, the couple bought a sixty-acre ranch north of Mountain Home near Canyon Creek not far from the historic Oregon Trail. There they raised nearly one hundred head of Black Angus cattle, grazing them on nearby Bureau of Land Management (BLM) and Forest Service (FS) lands. It was 1952,

Martha Ascuena on her horse Baldy near Featherville, Idaho, 1965. Courtesy of Martha Ascuena.

and at that time we had the telephone in our home that was connected with cross country [lines]. . . . Of course, we never called unless it was long distance. But it was one of the first telephones in that area. Of course, we didn't have neighbors that close, so that was one of the reasons I suppose. Remote, but oh, I loved it. It was just beautiful, down in our own valley by the creek.

The family spent thirteen satisfying years there, raising their two sons as well as cattle. In Martha's words, "It was a godsend for our two boys. They rode horses, drove truck; we never regretted that [raising them on a ranch]." Unfortunately, Jack's poor health forced the sale of this ranch in 1965, and the family moved into Mountain Home, where Ascuena took a job at the local hospital. Later, when I asked her about any difficult times she had experienced, her eyes filled with tears as she recalled those years when they had to leave the ranch for town. "My heart was still out on the farm," she told me sadly.

After Jack's death in 1969, friends introduced her to a widowed rancher named George Ascuena. His parents had immigrated to this country from their Basque homeland, Euskadi in northeastern Spain, and settled in Gooding in south central Idaho, prior to World War II. His parents farmed and his mother cooked for Basque sheepherders in a small local boardinghouse. After high school, Ascuena left for college in California and earned a teaching degree in Spanish. Returning to his roots in Idaho, he married a Basque woman from Mountain Home and secured a job teaching Spanish at the local high school. But farming was in his blood, and soon he began to build up a herd of Hereford cattle on about 200 acres east of this small Air Force town, in addition to his teaching job. George and his first wife raised a son and a daughter there before he was widowed in the early 1970s. As Martha explained, "I was a widow for five years, and during that period, George lost his wife. So a dear mutual friend of ours got us together and we came here in 1974. We were married and I moved out here." She continued to work at the hospital—"it was hectic trying to get things done out here and work in town"—until one day, George said, "'If you don't want to work at the hospital, why don't you just quit?' I did. . . . At that time his income and the ranch was enough to take care of things. So I thought, I could really be of more help to him out here than I could working." George understood her love of farming and, according to Martha, "Oh, everybody does. That's all I am is a farm lady. Yes, that's true. And that way I could kind of keep an eye on the cattle. In the winter time, keep the ice off the tanks and just little things that he wasn't here to do. And it worked out very well." As with so many other married couples in my study, the Ascuenas' shared labor provided a comfortable life centered on both ranching and George's wage labor as a teacher.

A shared sense of intimacy with a spouse or partner and the daily experience of enjoying the natural world appeared in many of my interviewees' comments. Carol Inouye of Parma, Idaho, described the outdoors life as "a very healthy experience and it just is a good way of life." Born in Canyon County in 1944, Inouye grew up in a farming family along with an older brother and a younger sister. "We just had a family farm, a 20-acre plot of land; by that time, in the late fifties, you couldn't support a family with 20 acres," so her father leased other parcels in the area and in Quincy, Washington, about a two-hour drive north of Parma. As they reached adulthood, her siblings did not consider farming a favorable career choice and left home for other lifestyles. Carol agreed with them, but marriage to a local Japanese American man changed her plans.

She told me an amusing story regarding how she ended up married to a farmer also with an ethnic name.

> I just was bound and determined not to marry somebody with a complicated name because my maiden name was Yamashita; and I was bound and determined not to marry into agriculture. I failed on both counts. You know, I think it [Inouye] has been even worse than Yamashita. But you know, the agricultural life was probably one of the best, looking [back] in retrospect, in which to raise a family. We had a very, very good life and lifestyle.

Carol was typical of many young women in the post-WWII era who finished high school then enrolled in college, in her case the College of Idaho in Caldwell. She enrolled in pre-med classes "not to be a doctor, but to be a medical lab technician; you've got to remember, this was the early sixties," she said, referring to the limited gender roles open to women then. She didn't finish college, however, preferring instead to date "the big, good-looking college man who came home" from Pocatello, where he was studying pharmacy at Idaho State University. Soon they married, she left college, and they "immediately had a family and farmed and the 'whole thing' started."

Her new husband had not intended to farm either, but after one year of pharmacy studies, "he had decided that no, it wasn't for him. He didn't like doing inside work, being inside; it was not very long before he realized he couldn't work inside, he was going to have to do outside work." So he returned to the family farm, and after their marriage in 1963, the couple rented a house on a farm near the extended Inouye family and were "just like any other farmer's hired workers," working not for themselves but for another family. A daughter and a son were soon born, and by 1973, they had an opportunity to buy a part of the family farm when one of Chris's uncles became ill and could no longer operate his acreage by himself. Since none of the uncle's children wanted to take over their portion of the family farm, Carol and Chris purchased the operation and continued to grow row crops, including sugar beets, potatoes, onions, wheat, and some mint, on leased land. But getting a loan to buy the farming operation was not an easy thing to do at that time, when many families were leaving the land due to high costs and low returns. Collateral was the problem.

We didn't have any collateral, we had nothing. We had just been renting a house for a couple of years and did try buying a house and were, at that time, trying to buy a house near Homedale. We had nothing else really. I think we owned one truck at the time, a 1972 truck. That is the extent of any collateral we would have had, so when we did decide to do this with the other uncle, we left Chris's father and uncle. Like I said, we worked quite hard and were quite disillusioned with what we were getting out of it. So we left them [her husband's father and brother] and found a bank, which at that time was Idaho First National Bank in Homedale, who would stick their neck out for us and with us. They gave us enough money to make payments and buy Chris's uncle out of his farming operation. It was a very large investment at the time; very great amounts of stress.

They bought his home and his equipment and entered into a share-cropping agreement, based on a handshake, with the landowner whose land the uncle had been farming. Quickly they were able to expand the initial 450 acres until they had leased 1,400 acres by the late 1990s, when they began to gradually cut back the size of their operation.

When I asked Carol if she did outside work in those early years, she said not much but, "I did a lot of things. I drove truck, I helped do all the things like burn weeds and do the small tractor jobs and run parts, run errands, and irrigate." Later, she described herself this way: "In a way, I considered myself a truck driver early on, because I didn't do very much tractor work, just little jobs with the tractor. I did quite a lot of irrigating and mostly truck driving." Then the children came along, and, as for other farmwives I interviewed, childcare and domestic duties soon dominated her daily routine, or as she put it earlier, "The 'whole thing' began."

All of the women I spoke with had children or stepchildren and uniformly declared that a farm is a great place to raise children. Doing things together is a way of life for agricultural families. No one "sleeps in" in these households. Children rise early to milk cows or do other chores before heading off to school and face more work when they return in the afternoon. Wives get breakfast for the family, put dinner in the Crock-Pot, and head out for the barn or fields. Over time, the shared experiences transcend into hardy values that bind family members together. Inouye spoke to the value of a work ethic when asked what made agriculture such a great lifestyle for raising children:

> Well, for one thing, whether this is good, bad, or indifferent, a definite work ethic can be instilled in children very easily on the farm. You just go out and work and it is there when you wake up. It's a little bit like housework—it is just there when you wake up. You just go out and do it. I suppose the children resented that a time or two, too—doing all of the work, but now that they are young adults and out on their own, they look back and can say, I'm sure with much sincerity, that they appreciate having learned how to work.

Family support networks are invaluable to agricultural families. Inouye spoke warmly of the advantage of living near both sets of parents, hers and her husband's, as they began their married life. "I was fortunate to have been in the same valley with both sets of parents . . . because of the help they could provide for raising children and just being a support for being a farmwife." During harsh times, such as the farm crisis of the 1980s, she drew on that support system.

> There were a number of times when I was quite distraught or the tension and stresses of borrowing so much money, being in debt [were] so horrible . . . very stressful, and so having the family networking is very important and I feel very fortunate to have had it. I can't imagine having done without . . . both the mother and the father part of that.

Born during WWII, Inouye grew up in a period of time that seems to have been quieter and safer.[18] Fears of kidnapping were not yet on parents' minds, the farm roads were less heavily traveled, and most Americans were still unaware of possible harmful environmental practices such as the use of pesticides or even the dangers inherent in unregulated fireworks use. She described her childhood this way: "I did enjoy being able to just ride my bike down the middle of the street in front of our house, . . . and liv[ing] out where I could set off fireworks and all of those things that children do . . . were definite perks, I suppose, to growing up in the country. . . . But, as a parent, and having raised children, I feel like it was the greatest."

Carol and Chris still live in the farmhouse they purchased in 1973. Although their children worked on the farm when they were growing up, they now live in other areas of the country. Carol believes the reasons for their departure stem from interests in careers other than agriculture. "With technologies and things growing so quickly in the last twenty years, it has been more glamorous than the farm." They are not alone in this situation; most daughters and sons view farming or ranching as hard, demanding work with little financial reward and choose not to stay on the land.

Helen Tiegs, of Nampa, did not grow up on a farm but would agree that raising children in the country is a positive way to shape young bodies and minds. Born in 1929, Tiegs has led a life that reflects the middle-class gender-based values of the times, that college was more important for a man and marriage was the eventual goal for women. Initially, her love of piano and the promise of a scholarship allowed her to study music at the College of Idaho in nearby Caldwell. At the same time, high school classmate Donald Tiegs was studying agriculture at the University of Idaho in Moscow, preparing to return to his family's farm. In her first semester, Helen discovered that college was not her priority.

> By the time I had gotten through the first semester, I knew that all I wanted to do was get married. And I was having a lot of fun in college—a cheerleader—I was really just not serious about college. So you know, in those days, it wasn't that important that a woman go to college, and I certainly did not take it seriously. And I thought, my parents cannot afford putting me through this college when I don't care any more about it than this. So I quit.

Their high school friendship grew into romance, then marriage in 1948; soon they purchased a homestead from the state land office for about $10 per acre, a good price but "it didn't have any water. We took the chance of drilling a well." She went on to describe the land, 10 miles south of Nampa in the Dry Lake area:

> When we moved out here, there was nothing but sagebrush, huge sagebrush . . . and we moved a little house out—about 12 by 20 feet—moved it over there. We didn't have any running water; we

didn't have any bathrooms. . . . We did have electricity, but we took our baths in the well that we drilled. . . . And I'll tell you what, my friends in town—I belonged to a bridge group—they could not believe this. "Old pioneer Helen! You're the only one that would do this." Of course, I kept telling Don, "I won't live out there without running water."

But she did, for at least six months, with three small children, all girls, in a one-bedroom house with outdoor plumbing. In the mid-1950s, they built a pumice, or concrete block, two-bedroom home; by then five children were sharing the second bedroom. When their family grew to six children (the three girls were followed by three boys), they built a larger permanent home, where Helen and her husband were still living when I interviewed her in her farm kitchen in 1995. During the visit, she showed me around the one-story ranch-style home and proudly pointed out the children's numerous school pictures gracing the walls.

My first impression of the Tiegses' farm on arrival that warm summer day in June was one of lush greenness covering the once sagebrush-dotted landscape. Silvery spray shooting from the pivot-point irrigation system punctuated the sunshine. Beautiful summer flowers framed the path from driveway to kitchen door, where Helen was waving me in. When I commented on the power of irrigation to alter the land so dramatically, she agreed.

> Yes, but we get our water from wells. We had to drill wells. We had a lot of people think we were crazy when we came out here. But that's what we did. And Don's brother—he lives south of us over there—he bought a couple of sections and Don bought a section and his dad bought a section over there . . . and that's how we watered. . . . All this land which is out in here, which is thousands of acres, are watered either from wells, deep wells, or water from the Snake River.

The Tiegs family farms are about 5 miles north of the Snake River, which runs east–west across southern Idaho, providing water for irrigation, electricity, and recreation all along its length. Helen went on to describe the large pumps built along the river that pump water uphill to the higher farmland. The Tiegses are members of the Hat Butte Co-operative, made up of area farmers who pay into the co-op, which buys water and electricity from the Idaho Power utility service. She went on to say that

> they all pay into it, and believe me, we pay a lot of money to the Idaho Power, a lot. And our wells cost a lot, too. That's all got to be paid for. It used to be, we used to have to pay thousands of dollars down every year before they'd even turn our pumps on. They don't do that now; I suppose that's maybe because they know we're reliable.

The Tiegses grow crops on their 400-plus acres; sugar beets and alfalfa seed are their two major crops. "We're kind of retired," she said, "or supposed to be. And our son raises peas for a company that are a real delicacy. And we raise wheat and barley and our son Dean raises corn, too, seed corn." Neither she nor her husband had worked off-farm, so when I asked if farming was their main way of life, Helen replied enthusiastically, "Oh, yes, I love it out here . . . it's a wonderful place to raise children."

One of those children, Helen's firstborn, Cynthia Tiegs Betz, agrees, although Cynthia was intent on moving off the farm by the time she became a young adult.[19] Born in 1949, she remembers moving to the dry land, digging the well, having no running water, and five more children coming along after her. As the oldest girl, she was the one who cooked and did things in the house, including caring for her younger brothers and sisters. "I was kind of mama's right hand; I didn't have to go out and irrigate and do those things, and I really didn't want to be a farmwife." After graduating from high school, she enrolled at the University of Idaho, where she met husband-to-be Eldon Betz, a sophomore majoring in education and agriculture. By the time he graduated in 1970, they had married, and Cynthia gave up college to be a wife and soon a mother. Whereas Cynthia did not choose to be a farmer or a farmwife, her husband was born to agriculture.

Eldon Betz was born in Greeley, Colorado, in 1948. His father, a sharecropper, moved the family to Fruitland, Idaho, when Eldon was four. Eldon remembers that their home had no indoor plumbing or heat but describes his childhood as good, based on "a lot of honorable skills." They "lived the old way"; his dad harvested with horses; his mother raised large gardens, canned the produce, and stored it in a root cellar. They also instilled a strong work ethic in their children; Eldon recalled his father's words: "'A handshake is a contract. You not only should honor it, but you will honor it to your death. It is as important as a signed piece of paper, probably more so. If you say you are going to do something, not only will you do it, you must do it.' And that's been in my head all this time." Eldon had a dual career as an educator and a farmer shaped by the values of keeping your word, being honest as well as honorable, and creating a shared and loving family presence as husband and father.

Upon graduation, Eldon secured a job teaching agriculture at Aberdeen High School, and the young family rented a farmstead 15 miles northeast of Pocatello, Idaho. The couple spent two years in eastern Idaho, then moved back to Moscow, where Eldon earned a master's degree in agriculture/education and a certificate in administration. For several months, he supported his family by working for the Cancer Society in northern Idaho. Then came a call from his father asking him to "come home and help with the family farm in Fruitland." So they returned to southeast Idaho, and Eldon began to farm with his father once again. Cynthia was not happy; Eldon told me that she "was quiet about this." According to Cynthia, she felt like a "reluctant farmwife when he wanted to farm. . . . It was always his thing, and I had to go out and just keep it up when he couldn't do it." After two months on the family farm and two offers to teach, the couple moved to Meridian, then a small community just west of Boise, and Eldon began to teach at Meridian High School. He also leased 80 acres nearby. And Cynthia's resentment grew.

> But my gosh, the thing I minded the most about it is he'd work long hours as it was; teaching professional agriculture is extremely—at least, the way he did it—time-consuming. He'd be working with kids till all hours of the night, painting tractors and whatever else they were doing down there. And then he'd come home and be out in the field until three or four in the morning sometimes. I wasn't real happy about that. So it was his thing.

But Eldon loved farming and felt it was a relaxing contrast to his work in the classroom. In his words:

> Here's academic and here's physical; being outdoors and the smell. I can remember sitting on a tractor on a Thursday night and it would

be one o'clock in the morning and everybody would be in bed and I'd be out there and it was cold and I'd look out and I'd see a fox in a stubble field. And I'd watch this fox; then I'd see a bird of prey land in a field and I just love that. And I love it when you cultivate a row and it's just perfect; there's no weeds and the smell of that soil . . . [voice trails off] And then, too, my dad was really important in my life and I just miss him, so it was [a] continuation of that too, partly.

Eldon echoes the sentiments of many of the farm women in this study who feel strongly about the virtues of farming and the close contact with nature it allows. And Cynthia acknowledges this as well, saying, "I did love the smell of the ground in the spring. And I like the smell of dairies actually, so I guess I'm a farm girl."

Once the family was resettled in Meridian, Cynthia enrolled part-time at Boise State University to earn a teaching degree. She finished in 1978, then began work on a master's degree in education, which she finished in 1986. She began teaching at the fourth-grade level, which she continues to do with as much commitment as Eldon has for his work teaching agriculture.

However, farming is not a stress-free occupation, and this farm family clearly experienced their share of stress. Both were teaching, Eldon was also farming and Cynthia was helping out, and they were raising a son and a daughter. Cynthia said that she "was proud that he was working so hard and doing so much but we did fight a lot about money and about expenses. Mostly because I wanted more security, ANY security, and you had NONE with farming." When Cynthia suggested to Eldon that he do one or the other but not both teach and farm, he reluctantly decided to give up farming. But it caused him "a lot of internal grief for two years; I really missed it a lot." He gave up teaching in 1992 and took a job with several seed companies for the next ten years. The work took him out of state for one or two weeks at a time, leaving Cynthia in charge. "[A]nd I could not keep things going. Invariably somebody would wreck something or something would go wrong, and I didn't know what to do." So he quit farming. In his words, "I didn't retire from teaching and I didn't retire from farming. I finally decided that my wife was correct and I either continue to work or I farm but doing both was just too much."

Those who work on and live on the land face numerous setbacks from time to time. Market prices and the weather are probably the two factors most beyond their control. Cynthia described the gambles they often had to take as more than spinning the wheel at a roulette table:

Then it [farming] was stressful because you didn't know—it was this huge gamble; it wasn't putting a buck down on the roulette table and you knew right away what was going to happen. You had to borrow money from the bank, . . . you didn't know what was going to happen. The weather would blow; that year it was the stupid beans—he had a wonderful bean crop—and it rained for two weeks and destroyed the crop. It makes my stomach hurt now, just because it was so scary, just chance. I saw that happen with my dad . . . so I hated that [element of farming].

Eventually, Eldon grew disenchanted working for the seed company and decided to go into business for himself. He became a distributor of drugs, medicines, supplements, and other products that veterinarians and animal owners require. It keeps him in contact with both agriculture and animals and allows him to create his own schedule. Cynthia loves teaching elementary school, fourth graders, and according to her husband, "she is a very strong promoter of the agricultural lifestyle in her classroom and always has been. She has done a lot of good, positive things for agriculture by doing that." Cynthia admitted that "a lot of times, I've felt, I'm glad I have that experience; I'm glad I can start a siphon tube. It's good to have had that in my background. [Although] I was kicking and screaming the whole way."

Growing up in agriculture but not wanting to be part of it is often a function of both parenting and education. As Cynthia noted earlier, she did not want to be a farmwife because she witnessed firsthand the difficulties her folks experienced. Yet Eldon was an early spokesperson for allowing high school girls to enroll in agriculture and shop classes, though it took many discussions with the administration to move attitudes away from traditional gender roles that said ag was for boys and home ec for girls. Finally, in 1973, Meridian High School allowed a few girls into their program. As it happened, the Betzes' daughter Robin flourished in vocational agriculture and served as president of FFA (Future Farmers of

America) in her senior year. Eldon is proud that his efforts made a difference in reshaping ideas around gender roles:

> The boys, for the most part, were very accepting. It forced them to be better because the girls would beat them, and it was really a kind of healthy and wholesome thing to watch. But the girls excelled in shop; they learned how to paint vehicles; they learned how to weld and do all those things. They put on the coveralls . . . jumped right in and got grease on themselves, and then they went out and did their cheerleading the next class period.

Eldon's support of young girls in agriculture was part of a larger movement taking shape in the 1970s, the renewal of the women's movement. In the next chapter, we will see how shifting gender roles were a part of farm and ranch life. For one young woman growing up in the 1980s and 1990s, living and studying ranching was just something she was born to.

On a beautiful autumn morning in October 2002, I interviewed two Colorado ranch women in the Upper Florida Valley, 20 miles northeast of Durango, a small city in the southwest corner of the state. Terra Graf, the youngest woman in my study at 24 years of age then, had come to visit her friend Marion Kelley and talk to me that morning at Marion's cattle ranch.[20] Terra was just 6 years old when their families became acquainted. The Graf family ran their cattle on BLM land above the Kelleys' ranch for many summers. Marion watched Terra grow up in the cattle business, and a caring friendship developed between the two that continues. They enjoy riding together—having "adventures," they call it—and today, Terra has brought her horse with her so the two women can ride after this interview. We begin talking outside in the ranch yard, where the several Kelley dogs are playfully vying for our attention.

While Terra grew up in the cattle business, Marion Kelley married into it, like Helen Tiegs. Marion was born in San Bernardino, California, shortly after the Pearl Harbor disaster in 1941. She told me that she wasn't exactly a city girl because "we kind of lived in the county. We had a few orange trees and three or four acres. It wasn't exactly the city."[21] She described the family lifestyle as "light agriculture" but added that she always liked animals, including horses, and helped her brother raise a calf. After high school, she met and married John Kelley, a welder and sheet-metal

Marion Kelley and Terra Graf on the Kelley Ranch in the Upper Florida River Valley east of Durango, Colorado, 2002. Courtesy of Marion Kelley and Terra Graf.

worker, skills that would be important later when they were ranching. When I asked how they got to Colorado, Marion said that even when she and John were dating, he spoke longingly of his grandparents' ranch there. He showed Marion summer vacation pictures and movies of the area, and she was smitten, too. "I liked it. And I always thought I'd like to be there. So after we were married, the first summer we came back here on vacation and I just loved this place. [I told John] we have to live there some day. So it took us until 1972 that we moved here. We love it." They married in 1962, and a son, Tim, was born four years later. He was 6 when they moved to the Kelley family ranch here in the Upper Florida Valley. At that time, John's family had leased the ranch to cattle people, so "we watched them and rode with them. It just gradually worked into [our] thinking that we should just have it for ourselves, and we gradually built a little herd of our own." John has been able to put his welding skills to good use on the ranch. Marion reported that he "kind of taught himself and just figured stuff out for [him]self. And usually it worked out." John keeps the equipment running, a skill Marion lacks, and also plays a role in running the cattle, putting up hay, taking part in the roundups, the brandings, and other seasonal jobs.

Farmland in the Lower Florida River Valley east of Durango, Colorado, fall 2002. Photo by author.

Terra's friendship with Marion evolved naturally from her mother's friendship with Marion through the years. Despite the difference in their ages, Marion and Terra share common interests and enjoy spending time together, especially on horseback. They recounted how, over the years, they have helped other ranchers round up their animals as well as pack salt blocks into the pastures five or six times a year. Together they explained this frequent ranch task.

> Terra: Yeh, packing salt is probably our biggest adventure. [laughter]
> Marion: You just pack the horses up, get them saddled, and put salt
>   blocks on them and start up the trail with it, ready for places
>   where the cows were used to coming to the salt and it's one of the
>   necessities, you know, [of] having ranch cattle, having salt blocks.

When I asked why salt is important, Terra responded:

> It's actually important just like minerals and vitamins [are] for
> you to have. And the salt's important for the cattle to have. But
> you also use it as a range management tool, and you put it in

places opposite of the water because the cow will travel across the land and actually utilize—of course, half the time they make big old mud puddles themselves, and so the cows just kind of just trample it in. [more laughter] But the idea is to keep them dispersed through[out] the range.

Marion: You spread 'em out so they utilize the pastures. You go from one to the other, and then water in between, and so they [ranchers] try to get them to come to different areas of the pasture to use the grasses that are better.

I ask how quickly the cattle use up the salt blocks.

Terra: We pack, what, five or six times a year? Well, it depends on if it rains a lot, too, because of course, it dissolves in the rain. And the wildlife use it as well.

Marion: Some of the areas they seem to go to more, and they will use that up sooner.

Terra: Sometimes we relocate the salt just because they tend to over-utilize that area. Most of the time we stay in the same area.

Born in Durango Community Hospital in 1978, Terra grew up realizing her parents' dream of living on a farm. "My dad and mom were both city people, and so they wanted to be out on the farm. That was really their dream. As kids, we just grew up with it."

Her parents dated in high school, were in 4-H together, and were captivated by ranch life in central Idaho where they spent several summers. After their marriage, they bought 40 acres north of Cortez, west of Durango, and began to raise heifers, increasing the herd each year. Terra's brother, ten years older, studied agricultural science and now teaches in the local school system. Terra rodeoed all four years in high school, was in 4-H for ten years, and even showed one of the Kelleys' steers one year at the 4-H fair. When she graduated from Montezuma/Cortez High School, she enrolled at Colorado State University with a concentration in animal science, "thinking I would maybe go to vet school, I don't know." But she left CSU after two years because "I kind of just wanted to be out and doing stuff for now. . . . It was nice to get back to something I knew."

I asked if she foresees a future in agriculture, and she was quick to tell me that she definitely plans to stay close to the land and animals.

Well, my dad is more into the production of cattle, and I'm more into riding horses and training horses for people. And of course, for some of the sporting competition, you have to have cattle, and so we would probably keep some around and train the horses with them. I would love to have a rehabilitation center for horses, but that's a long ways away, since I probably won't go to vet school. I'd probably just do a rehabilitation center or something to that effect with a neighbor already in the system. . . . I want to stay in the neighborhood . . . mainly dealing with cows and horses. We do some hay farming . . . so that we can feed the cows and not have to buy it. And we also sell some dairy production hay to dairies when we've got a good crop. Of course, this year we didn't [due to drought].

In 2000, Terra married Terrill Graf, a boy she knew in high school but didn't date. Then one fall when Terra returned to college in Fort Collins, Terrill followed her, literally, and a relationship developed that ended in marriage. Terrill had secured a job with a fertilizer company based in Nebraska that allowed him to live in Colorado while selling his products to ranchers and farmers there as well as in Kansas and Nebraska. After they married, Terra decided to leave college—she "just wanted to be outside doing stuff"—and they returned to the Cortez/Durango area. Terrill went to work for his parents' oil field service there. Like John Kelley, Terrill Graf is skilled in the mechanics of farm equipment and prefers hydraulics and electronics to animals, leaving most of the ranching chores to Terra.

When I spoke with Terra, the Grafs owned twenty-two mama cows; add in her dad's and brother's herds and, together, the families run a herd of about 170. And Terra added, "And then we always help the vet. He's the neighbor; he's got quite a few cows, and we help him and his brother out. And his nephews, so we kind of all just help each other out." This kind of cooperation is a common theme among the women I spoke with.

Before the interview ended, I asked both Terra and Marion how they feel about their chosen lifestyle. Graf spoke first: "I think it was neat growing up on a farm. You learn a lot of responsibility, mainly husbandry and just caring for human beings as well. If you can care for an animal, you can care for a human being." When I suggested a link between animals and nature, she agreed, saying, "Yes, there's a link to tending the land and tending the animals." Marion added, "Just kind of getting back to the basics, you know, of nature." Other women I spoke with share their attitudes. Carol Inouye expressed it this way: "I suppose one of the things about a farmer is that they do like to be outside in the fresh air." And Martha Ascuena told me that "when a person is working with the land, it's a feeling of accomplishment, if you enjoy doing it. And if you don't, you better not be there!"

For Carol Gildesgard, former hippie turned ranchwife turned prison corrections officer turned realtor in Reno, Nevada, the agricultural lifestyle is one she learned to love and hated to leave.[22] Born in Oklahoma City in 1945, Carol grew up in Los Angeles and attended a community college, where she met her first husband, Dale Ployhar, an aerospace engineer, whom she married in 1965. He first found work in the San Fernando Valley; then came a job in Santa Barbara. It was here in the mid-sixties that the young couple became, in Carol's words, hippies. They grew their hair long, attended rock concerts, and became interested in the health food movement, but they did not "do drugs," she told me. As the war in Vietnam heated up, they found themselves caught up in the excitement, the whole movement possibility. "It was an exciting time. It was depressing, though, because of the war, and I was not an antiwar protestor; I had no strong feeling because I was bogged down with children." Rather quickly, three baby boys had been born during this period. Then Dale became unemployed when the market for aerospace engineers declined in the late 1960s. Dale had grown up on a ranch in Montana, so his family suggested they move back and they would help the young couple financially. With that offer, they loaded up a U-Haul and headed north. Carol describes the move:

> So we drove back to Montana. The terrain changes as we cross the
> Divide; now we're in the Plains and we arrive in the Denton area,
> which is in the central part of the state, and moved in with the
> parents . . . on a farm which was mostly wheat and barley. It's all dry-
> land farming; you rely on the rain for irrigation. There's some cattle,

enough for feeding the families, but it was not a cattle operation. . . . We lived there about six months, which was hugely astounding to me because it's a very Catholic old Czechoslovakian family; the grandparents didn't speak English.

All the women were good cooks, and Carol described a custom in which they gathered in one home to make apple strudel. They moved the furniture out of one of the bedrooms, laid down a large cloth, and spread the dough out on the floor. Then family members tossed apples and cinnamon and raisins onto this stretched out dough, which

never seemed to stop stretching. Everybody was a good cook, all the women were overweight, and everybody prayed on their knees before a statue of Mary hanging on the wall in the corner. Now this was new to me; even though I was raised Catholic, that was not my lifestyle. But I blended in; I had to, and I was young and that was the beginning of my experience in this farm life—getting up early, staying up late, especially during the harvest season.

After about six months, they took over one of the other family ranches, numbering 1,800 acres, 20 miles north. Gradually, Carol learned the ways of ranch life.

I really got into the whole culture and digging in the earth and becoming a part of that and growing our own food. We never went to the grocery store but to buy toilet paper. We raised our own beef; we had a milk cow; I learned to milk a cow, which I wanted to do. There were chickens; that was interesting for me because I hadn't really done those kinds of things before. I never could butcher a chicken. Anna [a neighbor] would come over and slit their throats, and then we would butcher. And my husband made me stick my hand in the chicken innards and pull it out, not just what you get at the grocery store now. Usually, we'd have a fight about that, too. And he'd say, "You have to learn how to do this," and I did.

The family moved into an old farmhouse that had once been a showplace. While it had electricity and running water, it lacked a clothes dryer, a dishwasher, and a shower. She hung clothes (lots of diapers) on the line, where they would freeze in the Montana winters. She learned to churn butter in her Mixmaster; her husband rigged a shower for her with a faucet and a clothes hanger. She found she loved to cook and said, "I had *Farm Journal* cookbooks and taught myself. I was always in the kitchen, always on my feet with a baby on my hip." In the middle of the Montana plains, they had little television reception, just two stations, one in Billings, one in Great Falls. Her husband tied a rope to the rooftop antenna and "when I wanted to watch a soap opera, I went out and pulled the rope and rotated the antenna and tied it to another tree to watch the show in Billings." Like many another farmwife, Carol used creativity and resourcefulness to manage life under challenging conditions.

Winters were difficult. "I'd look out the window and just see the white skies and the white fields and it was intensely boring and I was lonely and the family wasn't around. The first couple of years were really tough; and all these babies [a fourth son had been born since they moved to Montana] and I'm depressed." Eventually, she told herself, "This is it, this is where I'm going to be; I'd better make the most of it. I had the joy of learning to cook and was excited about that; learned to can, grow gardens, raise chickens. I learned it OTJ [on the job]."

Finally the weather; she wanted to talk about the weather:

> Winters are so intense, I can barely describe it. The cold, the storms, the howling of the wind for days on end. And we were on the Plains; a lot of the people on the west side of the Divide didn't experience that kind of barrage; they have heavy weather, to be sure, but this howling, driving wind all the time, always the wind. But I liked the wind. In the winter it got pretty sad; you'd get cabin fever. . . . Very extremes of weather. Depression, yes, but we were busy and were raising a young family; we didn't have time to be depressed. . . . You can't be weak in Montana. So everybody was strong, outwardly strong.

It may be a cliché to stereotype farmers and ranchers as strong and resilient, but the very nature of their profession demands such traits. I heard it in the stories my interviewees told me and sensed a modest kind of satisfaction in the telling. Most often, they cited the positive outcome of raising children who learned early the value of hard work, sacrifice, and perseverance. Felicia Thal, a New Mexico woman we will meet in the next chapter, moved to a ranch with her husband, two teenagers, and a 5-year-old in 1972. She believes that "we did more for our children by turning to the ranching way of life than anything else we ever did. It gave our family a unity of purpose."[23] Thal and the others spoke of the strong connection they feel between themselves and nature itself, treasuring those moments when the long-awaited spring rains trigger the appearance of shiny green-tipped leaves of corn in long, geometrically plowed rows, the silhouette of a windmill framed by a pastel sunset, or freshly canned jars of the garden's riches lined up on pantry shelves. They spoke also, usually hesitatingly, of stressful times, as Carol Gildesgard did, when storms flattened the wheat, of the breakdown of expensive equipment or the nearly overwhelming debt that engulfed so many families in the past three decades.

These were difficult periods that tested their fortitude, their decisions, and sometimes their marriages. Such situations forced many families to find creative ways to maintain their lifestyle. Since at least the 1950s, the most common solution has been the decision for one of the partners to work off-farm to ease the financial pressure. More recently, some owners, particularly ranchers, rent their land and its assets to the public for recreational activities, such as hunting or fishing. Sometimes this decision stemmed from necessity, such as the death of a spouse and the need for more income. Often these choices reflect a flexibility in gender roles in the farm couple. Perhaps this flexibility is visible in agriculture more than other kinds of work since the structure of farming, by its nature, requires family labor. In chapter 2, my informants talk about their relationships not just with the land but with their spouses/partners and how these relationships shaped, consciously or not, their daily lives, working the land.

2

"I'd Rather Work Outside Than Do Housework"

Flexible Gender Roles

"Memories of my grandfather's death were tied to another small death, the day I discovered that as a girl, I would never own my childhood ranch," wrote Judy Blunt in her 2002 bestseller *Breaking Clean*.[1] Blunt's gritty yet graceful memoir of growing up on the prairies of eastern Montana in the 1950s reflects the reality of the patriarchal nature of agriculture, that the boys in the family had a chance to inherit, but the girls did not. "In our family the sons would follow the father; Kenny the elder, would have first refusal. We girls would be left something of value, but we should know at the outset that we would never inherit the land."[2] Blunt's parents were third-generation homesteaders who staked out their claims near the small town of Malta, 50 miles or so south of the Canada-Montana border. There, on the dusty hardpan and sagebrush flats, they raised cattle and grew wheat. Blunt and her four siblings learned the value of hard work from their parents, hardscrabble people who counted on the labor of their five children for survival. Blunt recounts that "I could rope and ride and jockey a John Deere as well as my brothers, but being female, I also learned to bake bread and can vegetables and reserve my opinion when the men were talking."[3] She also grew up with a set of rules and roles that were prescribed for her sex long before she was born and that ultimately forced her to make a choice: she could marry or she could leave. Choosing marriage to a neighboring rancher, she stayed until she could stand it no longer, finally fleeing the ranch and her marriage after fourteen years.

By her teen years, Blunt had become a wise observer of both the physical and mental worlds around her and had subconsciously noted changes on the landscape and to surrounding family farms and ranches.

Beginning in the late 1960s, land values began to rise, making small family farms worth more than ever and retirement an attractive proposition to many. Coupled with rapid improvements in farm technology and the growth of agribusiness, change came to farmland nationwide, triggering enormous social and economic pressures. In Blunt's community, population shrunk by a third as small, marginal operations were absorbed by larger ones. Those farm families without children, or children willing to remain in agriculture, sold out to those who had sons ready to take over the family place. Blunt's older brother Kenny had studied modern agribusiness practices in college and was made a partner when her parents purchased a second ranch and incorporated as Blunt Ranches, Inc., in 1962. She recalled, "Overnight, it seemed, the place I grew up on had fallen under the wheels of big business—big land, big lease, big machines. Big debt. . . . And I had no place in the new dealings."[4]

Blunt's dilemma is not a new development in ranching, given the patriarchal nature of agriculture. Historically, the male has served as the dominant actor on the farm or ranch. The contributions of women to the enterprise have been overlooked by both government policies that recognize the male as decision maker and social-cultural attitudes that reinforce this practice. For example, women often serve as mediators between fathers and sons in order to ensure the continuity of farming as a way of life and the intergenerational transfer of family enterprises.[5] The wife looks to her son(s) to assume ownership of the property rather than attempt to claim it in her name. More often, upon a husband's death, his will allows her to remain on the property until her death, at which time it would then pass to the male heir. Sons most often inherited management of the land, went into partnerships with their fathers, or received the father's financial support in starting their own farming operations. These opportunities were not available to most women, as Judy Blunt painfully discovered. If a daughter inherited the family farm, or some portion of it, rarely did she step into management of the property. More likely, she became an absentee landowner or she remained on the farm but designated a husband or male relative as farm manager.[6]

Underlying these patriarchal practices are clear gender expectations. Postwar domestic ideology confined women primarily to housework and childcare, an ideology constructed for white middle-class women. The quote used in this chapter title suggests that this woman has some degree of choice and would "rather" work outside the home. Such a choice would not be possible for poor or working-class rural women. Lack of economic resources dictates that more often, she has no choice in how she spends her day, indoors or outdoors. In this way, women's farmwork is often overlooked because it appears that she is just "helping out" and can return to the kitchen when the task is complete. Often it is not a matter of choice. If the family cannot afford to hire labor, the unpaid labor of wives is expected. In this way, gender roles are quite fluid when it comes to what is expected of women. They are less fluid when household chores are the issues; husbands are less willing to do the laundry or make beds while the wife is harvesting beans.

Rosalie Romero, from the small village of Chacón in northern New Mexico, provides an example of working-class expectations.[7] She wasn't quite fifteen when she became pregnant and married the father, Alfonso Romero, in 1949. The couple had been married forty-six years when I interviewed her in 1995. From the beginning, Rosalie always worked, formally off-ranch for wages and periodically on their sheep ranch. As is common among ranch and farm families and especially the Hispanic families in this valley, they initially worked his father's land; now they and their children farm 800 acres. When their first child was six months old, Alfonso followed other farm laborers north to pick potatoes in fields around Monte Vista in southern Colorado. Rosalie had no choice but to work both in the fields and in the farmhouse; her mother-in-law provided childcare. Electricity came to this isolated valley in 1946, but her family's source of water was the nearby river; outdoor plumbing was the norm. Not until 1982 did they get running water in their house. Despite a life of hard work in the fields, in the home, and in town, Rosalie retains a cheerful personality and a sense of optimism. She is an example of a rural working-class woman who did what was expected of her within gender and class parameters. She also found personal satisfaction through the many ways she helped support her family.

In west Texas, self-defined agribusiness woman Jean Nichols was more than willing—in fact, determined—to bend traditional gender boundaries. When I interviewed Jean on her farm in Idalou, 10 miles northeast of Lubbock, she had been farming with her husband, Dean, for thirty-four years. Her greatest wish growing up on her family's farm was to own and run her own operation. Not true for her two sisters, but for Jean, "The

Rosalie Romero on the porch of her home, Chacón, New Mexico, 1995. Courtesy of Rosalie Romero.

only thing I ever wanted to do was farm. But that was not—my daddy let me know that was not something a woman did."[8] Despite wanting to major in agriculture at Texas Tech University, she earned a degree in education in 1964 and began teaching biology and coaching a softball team in nearby Friendship, Texas. Her future husband's sister was the team pitcher, and as she put it, "Dean was single and I felt an attraction to him." By this time, her dad wanted to leave farming and because "my daddy wouldn't let me have my farm . . . and I didn't want to not have the farm," she and Dean married in 1967. One year later, they bought the farm from Jean's father. When I asked her if this had been a marriage of convenience, she answered, "One could possibly say that for more reasons than one, yes." I probed a little deeper: "To secure the land for you?" To which she replied: "That was the only way I was going to get it."

As I spent the day driving around the west Texas farmscape with Jean, I came to appreciate how this sturdy, determined farmer had shaped her life around agriculture. After marriage, she continued her education, earning a master's degree in physical education in 1973 and began work on a PhD in psychology. Then, she told me, "I was going good with that and got pregnant and you know, shifted roles. . . . The marriage was rocky but I said, no, this is what I'm going to do for my daughter and make sure that she has two parents." For the next several years, Jean did the requisite parental and community activities while still farming with her husband. She served on the boards of several Lubbock community organizations, including the Garden and Arts Center and the Lubbock Art Association, served as president of PTA for seven years, then was elected to the local school board in Idalou. During her tenure on the school board, she became interested in planning issues, which led her to think about the role nearby Texas Tech could play in rural schools. As a result of her inquiries, she became aware of the Land Use Planning Management Design Program, and that provided the focus for her PhD work; she earned her degree in May 2001. She described her project as about the "environment and natural resources . . . so it's primarily agriculture but from a different standpoint." Initially denied ownership of family farmland, Jean has negotiated and crafted a life built around both family and agriculture. In addition, her higher-education achievement has provided a professional edge and brought her great satisfaction. Nichols's life represents what historian William Chafe refers to as a "paradox of change."

In his overview of American women in the twentieth century, Chafe characterizes the post–World War II period as a seeming paradox for women and, hence, for society in general.[9] Once World War II ended and the soldiers began streaming back home to take up their civilian lives once again, the wartime "Rosies" and "Wandas" were laid off or were fired to make room for the returning men. Yet they did not stay home long but quickly returned to the workplace, not in their former skilled jobs but in the traditionally female "pink-collar" sector as secretaries, teachers, nurses, and librarians and in certain female-centered factory jobs such as textiles and food manufacturing. As the number of women in the workplace increased in the 1950s and 1960s and into the 1970s, it became clear that women were willing to leave "their sphere" to work outside the home for wages but did not necessarily see themselves as feminists or as part of the newly revived women's movement. On one level, gender roles were in flux, yet most Americans still considered males as the breadwinning head of the family and females as caretakers of home and nurturers of children. Chafe refers to this situation as a "strange paradox."[10]

Cynthia Tiegs Betz found herself caught in this period of shifting gender roles. She described her family's style this way: "In our traditional family, I appreciated my mom being home full-time. In our family, there was a huge division of labor. Daddy did all the outside stuff and all of the farming; Mama did not do that. And that's another reason I probably resented having to go out and help Eldon [her husband]; I never really saw my mom go out and help at all. I was raised with all those stereotypes of men and women and what they do." As for her husband, Eldon saw his dad as the sole provider and thought that was the way it should be—no sharing of the wage-earning role. His father's example shaped his ideas of how a marriage should be structured.

By the seventies, when Cynthia and Eldon were in college, Cynthia became aware of other possibilities suggested by the growing women's movement. "I had gotten involved in it at the U of I. Bra burning—I wasn't into that, but we were becoming very aware, we were becoming more aware.... I must have been a burgeoning feminist because I wouldn't have taken, what was it —home ec?—for all the tea in China! I knew it wasn't anything I wanted to do."

She had seen how hard it had been for her parents and knew that she "never wanted to live like that." Instinctively, she rejected the traditional gender roles she had been raised with.

> I had always felt that it was unfair when I was growing up that all I got to do was sew for 4-H and cook. And I hated sewing; cooking was OK, but I couldn't have an animal, like all the boys had animals. I would have liked to have [had] that.... I became more aware as we were in college and thought about some of those things because it was in the forefront about women and about how unfairly we had been treated. I really felt this and I could see it more and more all the time.

In their marriage, Cynthia and Eldon generally talked over major decisions and came to agreement. On one occasion, however, Eldon surprised her with a new piece of equipment. "I remember the day he came home with a $14,000 tractor. I don't know when I've been so mad! We didn't [talk that over ahead of time] and we were living here and you know, he said then—I think it was more than $14,000 by the time he got tires put on it, right?" Eldon went on to explain how, in the end, they got their money out of the tractor when they later sold it for a newer one with a cab, a heater, and air conditioning. When I asked Cynthia how

Cynthia Tiegs Betz and her pack goats, Meridian, Idaho, 2004. Courtesy of Cynthia Tiegs Betz.

she handled major purchases, she replied, "Actually if I needed something, usually we would talk it over, but I've been pretty autonomous with money as well over the years. But no $14,000 purchases that I can remember!"

Although Cynthia's father raised his family according to traditional sex roles, he also understood that a life of domesticity might not provide enough security for his daughters. He therefore advised Cynthia and her sisters to go to college in order to have a fall-back position, one that would allow for self-sufficiency should a breadwinner husband fail in his role as head of the family. Cynthia explained that

> Daddy had told the three girls, my sisters and I, that you know, you need to get a college degree; you never know what might happen. Your husband might die or you just don't know. So you can be a nurse or you can be a secretary or you can be a teacher. [laughter] My middle sister is a nurse, my younger sister . . . started out as a secretary; and I became a teacher. We were just programmed and we followed right through.

When I asked if her dad had offered his daughters a chance to farm with his sons, Cynthia replied, "Oh no. I'd have been flummoxed if he had ever suggested such a thing. No. Belinda and Marsha would have been, too." And yet, she married a man who loved to farm and regretted she had not been allowed to experience farming as a child growing up in agriculture. Nor could she have known of the enormous social changes ahead, a period in which the women's movement would provide a new world of possibilities for girls and women.

As an economic organization, the family farm is a close-knit unit in which family members work together to ensure the operation's survival. Yet the traditional image of women on farms depicts them as helpmates whose labor is only indirectly related to agriculture and is centered primarily on domestic chores. As we have seen, this image is changing. Some agricultural women do drive tractors and other specialized equipment and work at traditionally male tasks as part of their daily labors. While this is a complex issue, research suggests at least three reasons for this shift across traditional gender lines: (1) the measure of power and satisfaction such work brings, (2) a closer and more equitable relationship with a spouse, and (3) a preference for working outdoors—all reasons that appear in my informants' comments.

As we will see in the next chapter, farm women frequently leave the home sphere to work for wages to augment farm income. While they primarily see their efforts as another variation of serving as a helpmate, some women and men willingly exchange gender roles to better serve their families' needs. This practice was not uncommon among my interviewees, particularly Kali Holtschlag, a ranch woman in southeastern Arizona. I interviewed Kali in her ranch kitchen on the Adams Ranch, 15 miles east of Benson, on a sunny morning in May 1996.[11] Kali was born in Flagstaff in 1959, a fifth-generation Arizonan whose parents left the family ranch and became anthropologists and urbanists. Raised mostly in Arizona, Kali and her siblings spent many summers on her grandparents' ranch. As she tells it, ranching skipped a generation in her family:

My mother kind of left. It's kind of funny; I see this in several families I know. There's kind of an alternation of generations; if they can hold onto the ranch, the grandkids will come back. My mother—there was a story that just killed me when I was young.

She traded her horse for a bicycle, and I was the other way around. I would have given, you know, ten bicycles for a horse, growing up in town. So she went into anthropology and fine arts at the University of Arizona and met my dad and kind of left the ranch.

Still, Kali's mother kept her hand in the ranch business, taking care of the books, as her mother had done, and preparing the taxes. Kali graduated from high school in Scottsdale, then attended Arizona State University for two years before transferring to the University of Arizona to study in the Department of Ecology and Evolutionary Biology. After a year and a half, she met Mike Holtschlag; they soon married, and she left the university. Mike and his dad are stonemasons, and Mike has continued in his father's business, leaving Kali to be the rancher. One son was born in 1985 when they lived in Tucson; in 1986 they moved to the ranch. Explaining her ties to the family ranch, she told me, "I was the oldest; I was my grandfather's pet, so that's probably how I got more connected with the riding and that sort of thing." Kali's grandmother had died in 1976, and within ten years, her grandfather had become senile and no longer able to ranch for himself. She describes this as a difficult period because

for about three or four years, well, actually there was about a seven- or eight-year period when almost nothing was getting done. Grandpa was an old cowboy and he carried a gun around and you didn't help much. You didn't mess around with the cattle; he couldn't do it, and it was really rough. . . . He was the boss, they were his animals and his place and you just didn't cross him. So what we did was, the cattle just sort of, were on their own for several years.

The family took care of Grandpa Adams until his death in 1989, a month after her second son was born. Mike continued to work the masonry business, now mainly in Benson, and Kali took over the management of the ranch. Because her husband is, as she describes, "not really a rancher," she called on her cousin, Mike Mercer, who is "really good. He's a young man, but he just kind of knows the old-time ways and he decided he wanted to do this and he went out and learned how to do it." While both men serve in typical male breadwinner roles, it is Kali who has crossed gender lines to take on essentially the full management of the ranch. In fact, speaking of Mercer's needing assistance, she told me, "If I just had the guts, I'm sure I could do it by myself."

That statement led me to ask Kali how she identifies herself on census forms; she responded in this way: "Oh, sometimes I write foreman and sometimes I just write rancher. When grandpa was there, I was a caregiver." She emphatically stated that she is "not a housewife. I prefer to be outdoors. My husband says, 'Anything but the dishes,' right? 'I'll do anything [but that chore].'" When I visited Kali, she had a new dishwasher, a Christmas gift from her mother and greatly appreciated.

> I've been here ten years and hand-washing for ten years. My husband is very good; he's good with the children, he's not a traditional kind of male that won't do housekeeping or cleaning or cooking. He cooks and cleans when he can, too. . . . We share these things pretty well. I do most of the ranching things; he does, I mean, he helps where he can but he doesn't know it and doesn't have that—you know, you have to feed the horses; you have to do these things, there's no question about it. He doesn't have that. The cattle come first; he doesn't have that, either. That's OK, that's not his thing, but sometimes that's a conflict. . . . Because he doesn't understand why the cattle have to come before the family sometimes. Like I said, he's a stonemason; his dad was.

As one might expect, making decisions about ranch management falls to Kali, her cousin, and, for awhile, her mother. Speaking of her mother's role, Kali told me that

> Mother and I, we worked really well as a team. It was kind of like, just through conversation we would decide to do something. It wasn't—it was kind of how teams should work; the communication was almost nonverbal and now, she just passed away in February, now it's different. It's really different with my father. But probably, it's probably mostly my decisions, as far as the ranch goes. As far as day-to-day things, just kind of like I said, [it] depends on what needs to get done. Just do it.

As so often happened with this study, one ranch woman led me to another, and it was Kali who suggested that I meet and visit with one of her neighbors, Peggy Monzingo, who also had been recommended to me by Editha Bartley in New Mexico. Both women are or have been in the bed-and-breakfast business, so I made arrangements with Peggy to stay overnight at her ranch, 20 miles north of Benson, after finishing the interview at the Adams Ranch. Peggy is an avid activist in the cattle industry, the subject of chapter 5, and before I turned on my tape recorder the next morning, she made sure she served me breakfast, then met an 8 AM deadline for sending off a fax.

Once settled at her large oak dining table, Peggy, who married into ranching, described her life to me.[12] She was born in 1922 in St. Louis, and the family moved to Chicago when she was in her teens; however, she was sent to boarding school in Dobbs Ferry, New York, where she excelled in sports and became interested in drama and art. After graduation and a trip to Italy just prior to World War II, she returned to the States and entered Vassar College, with art as her major. However, Peggy wasn't completely committed to this path; she told me that "Pearl Harbor became a very good excuse to quit college, so I went back to Winnetka [a suburb north of Chicago] and worked in a private school as a secretary during the war." During this period she met her first husband through a mutual friend; he was in training for the Coast Guard at that time, so they corresponded and subsequently married in 1942 in California. Their honeymoon site, on his cattle ranch in Patagonia, Arizona, introduced her to her life's work thereafter. In her words, "I adored the country. I adored the work." And no, she "had no training for it."

Her new father-in-law and a cowboy were running the ranch until her husband returned, which wasn't until V-J Day in August 1945. A daughter was born in 1946, and Peggy quickly learned what ranch work required and how to build up a herd of registered cattle. Horses had always been a part of her life, albeit at livery stables during her childhood, but she had also visited the West on a family vacation as a 9-year-old, when they stayed at a dude ranch in Nevada. Over the next decade, her husband turned more and more of the ranch chores over to her and began teaching school. Peggy again: "He was supposedly cowboying, but he didn't really like it as much as I did."

By 1960, the couple had been separated for two years, and Peggy "had been running the ranch alone for over two years." In the divorce that followed, she kept half the herd they had built up and moved them to a ranch, about 10,000 acres, they had purchased south of Santa Rosa, New Mexico, in the 1950s. She and her teenaged daughter settled in and began to build up the herd once more.

In 1964, Peggy married again. Ed Monzingo had been the foreman on the ranch in Patagonia, and over the years they had worked long hours together and become friends. They were married on the new ranch, a marriage that lasted twenty-four years, until Ed's death in 1988. Peggy described those years as being

> as wonderful as anybody could ever hope for, so I don't feel I have been cheated in life at all, just because of one bad step in the beginning. . . . We were completely compatible; my belief really jelled there that the marriages that are based on friendship and respect, before you fall in love, are the ones that work because we had worked together for years [on the Arizona ranch and] we were focused. We thoroughly enjoyed our challenges and our efforts to get on top of them and so forth.

Peggy credits Ed with teaching her the basics of ranching, describing it this way:

> I learned what I know about cowboying basically from working with him. . . . It has been my entire life; I'm a cow person . . . I am interested in the cattle and I am sorry that I had to give up riding; my knees got too bad. Basically, I've had over fifty years of working on ranches in the Southwest that are involved in federal and state lands. I'm proud of it, and I love it. It's been my whole life . . . the just plain nitty-gritty cowboying; it has been an absolute focus and absorption in my life.

When I suggested she had always been the one to "call the shots" on the ranch, she replied:

> Not always. For the two years that I was separated before my divorce, in the 1950s I was; [and] for the period between my divorce and remarrying, I was; [and] since widowhood, I am, but that is really a

false assumption because always there was a knowledgeable, savvy cowman in the picture for me. The man working on the ranch out at Patagonia was able to just get my input on "can we afford to do this" or "this is what it would do," and I learned through that process. Same thing when we moved and started the ranch in New Mexico. I had him for the cow savvy part and I was able to meld that with what I had learned about bookkeeping and so forth and so on and do my share on that as much as on the cowboying end—but now my son has evolved into a knowledgeable, observant . . . he is becoming a cowman like his father, and while he thinks he ought to be as good as his father was at 77, he is only 29. He has a way to go, but he has made tremendous strides in thinking through problems and [is] savvy about maintenance and vehicles and cattle, learning them. You don't learn cattle out of a book, and you don't learn until you are doing it, and for about five or six years, he has been doing it and he has made tremendous strides and I'm just terribly proud.

The women in this chapter are no shrinking violets, as we can see. They don't shirk hard work; indeed, they realize it comes with the territory. It was not always this way, however. In the early twentieth century, when thousands of farm families were leaving their land and migrating to cities, agricultural reformers devised plans to halt or at least slow down this rural to urban migration. They believed that if hard physical labor could be removed from farmwork, farm folk would acquire a new middle-class status. Men would use technology and brains rather than brawn to work their farms. Improved domestic technology in the form of labor-saving devices—vacuum cleaners, automatic washing machines, and later, home freezers—would create professional homemakers, relieving women of the "drudgery" of domestic farm labor.[13] In the postwar years, this message did help transform the image of the family farm, but most farmwives did not rush to embrace a new professional domestic identity. Those who chose to work in the fields or with animals continued to do so and benefitted from the increasing and improving technology their husbands also enjoyed.

In a rapidly globalizing world, farming has become a profession that requires more technology and specialized knowledge. Rural life no longer calls up images of isolated farm families doing without modern

Rangeland, northern New Mexico. Photo by author.

conveniences. Good roads, electricity, running water, and consumer goods made life easier and more comfortable. For some time, rural people have had access to the same comforts and consumer items as city people; they wear the same kinds of clothes, read the same magazines and newspapers, watch the same television programs and movies, and generally have life-styles similar to urbanites'. While many of these changes occurred prior to World War II, the war accelerated technological change, and television came to shape social and cultural behavior. As more women gained access to family vehicles, the rural woman in her pickup truck became as familiar an image as the suburban mom in her station wagon or the soccer mom in her SUV later. No longer are rural families considered deprived because they live in the countryside.

Increasing mechanization and a declining need for hired laborers meant that more farm women found themselves in the tractor's seat. In 1958, the farm journal *Wallaces' Farmer* polled farm families "to determine the extent to which farm men and women were crossing traditional gender-role boundaries to 'help' each other with farm or housework."

Seventy-seven percent of men reported that their wives drove a tractor or helped with livestock. Studies done in the Midwest in 1962, in 1979, and in the 1980 National Farm Women Survey indicate increasing numbers of women doing outside farmwork. The 1980 study of 2,500 women and 500 men showed that 17 percent of the women regularly did some fieldwork that did not require machinery; 11 percent plowed, disked, cultivated, or planted as a regular duty; and 5 percent regularly applied fertilizers, herbicides, or insecticides (which often is done with machinery). On farms where fieldwork was done, a large proportion of women reported taking part at least occasionally, part of the shift toward fieldwork being more acceptable gender-role behavior.[14]

There were generational differences, however, that suggest changing gender-role expectations. Young women between the ages of 20 and 34 were more likely to do fieldwork than women older than 50. *Wallaces' Farmer* editor Zoe Murphy reasoned the difference existed because "an older woman can't swing up on a tractor as easy as a young one."[15] Some women did not let awkward equipment stand in their way of fieldwork, however. In Carolyn Sachs's 1970s study, *The Invisible Farmers,* one of her respondents recounts that when her doctor suggested that driving a tractor might be the cause of her medical problems, she refused to believe "that women weren't made to ride tractors"; rather, "tractors weren't made for women."[16] Rather than give up fieldwork, which she took great pride in, she adapted the equipment to her needs; she rebuilt the seat to make it more accessible to the pedals and levers. Improved technology along with changing gender expectations have allowed women to move outdoors while still retaining a domestic role within the home.

Elizabeth Lloyd was one such woman. When her farm family moved from eastern Idaho to eastern Oregon in 1946, she and her husband farmed with a team of horses until they could afford to invest in a tractor. Lloyd, who preferred to work outside rather than inside the farmhouse, "did everything that men did.... [She] worked on the combine, tied stacks, pitched hay, drove a tractor, operated equipment." Growing up as the only girl with five brothers, Lloyd described herself as a "tomboy"— one who would rather milk cows than do housework, and whose parents allowed her the freedom to do so. It was a natural transition when she married to continue to do outside work, not only because it was work she knew and loved but because her labor was an important economic

Ramona Martinez, her husband, and three sons farm several hundred acres in the Mora Valley in northern New Mexico. Here Ramona and sons repair equipment in the field, Mora, New Mexico. Courtesy of Ramona Martinez.

contribution to the farm operation. In addition, it brought her a measure of status and prestige that no amount of housekeeping could provide.[17]

Lloyd's experiences suggest a less tangible but no less important factor that attracts women to outside farm tasks: the satisfaction of working with spouses. Lloyd had a close working relationship with her husband, which meant "we did most things together," and she took pride in being "the only help he had." Martha Ascuena spoke of the pleasure as well as the expectation that she would work outdoors with her husband and two sons, saying, "Generally if you saw one of us, you saw four of us; my husband, myself, and the two boys."[18]

Linda Murgoitio, a self-defined farmer in Meridian, Idaho, contrasted her earlier off-farm employment with outside farmwork.[19] When asked if she would work off-farm again, perhaps when their two children were grown, she was hesitant to commit to the possibility, preferring to maintain the warm partnership she and her husband Gary have created. She went on to say, "When I was working outside the home I think my relationship with Gary suffered. Gary and I are terribly close now, and I don't want to jeopardize [that by] going back [to work]. . . . I really like hanging out with him and doing whatever he's doing. . . . We seem to be pretty close."

While Murgoitio emphasizes her outside work and partnership with her husband as integral to the family's labor system, she is less aware of her role in reinforcing the patriarchal structure of their family farm. She is still the primary caretaker of their children, so her labor is difficult to separate into tidy gender-based spheres. Yet her willingness to combine household management, childcare, and farming can strengthen the operation. According to historian Sarah Elbert, "Indeed, in times of crisis, the farming family's willingness to shift gender roles, to split time between on- and off-farm work, and to share child care often saves the family farm."[20]

Editha Bartley, ranchwife and manager of the Gascón family ranch near Las Vegas, New Mexico, echoes Murgoitio's spousal commitment when she recounts the forty-one-year "incredible partnership" she had with her husband, Jim, until his death in 1991. "You learn to share and communicate when you're working like this. . . . We consulted with each other on almost everything." Over the years, Bartley learned all aspects of cattle ranching, tasks that have been crucial to the family's economic well-being both while her husband was living and since his death. Each partner relied on the labor of the other, appreciating his or her special strengths. She comments:

> I usually called the shots on the cattle, what cows to sell or something like that. I love working with cattle, and he left it up to me. I kept all the records and still do. . . . If I said we should sell a cow, or not sell a cow, I'd give my reasons, then he'd give his, and we'd come to a meeting of the minds. We always reasoned it out. He never got in my way either.

Drawing lines between men's and women's work was less important than carrying out the work of the ranch; the Bartleys were partners in a joint venture based on a balance of power, an example of the flexibility in gender-role behavior they practiced. New Mexico ranch women like Editha share a common lifestyle with their Texas counterparts.

The lifestyle of the rancher, notes sociologist Elizabeth Maret, has always been highly romanticized.[21] Indeed, the cattle rancher and his "posse" of cowboys is a standard part of the myth of the West. Combining the quantitative tools of the sociologist and the oral history methods of historians, Maret determined to uncover the roles women played in this highly masculinized industry in Texas, where every statistic connected with beef cattle dominates the industry nationwide.[22] Ranching, like farming, is a family-based enterprise; hence, where there are women, they are contributing to the overall success or failure of the operation. Her book is rich with details of women's presence in ranching, insights that fit several of my subjects also. Nudging aside the stereotype of the male rancher, Maret found women and men working alongside one another to be the norm both historically and in the present.[23] They see themselves as farm women do, as "go-fers"; they share in decision making with spouses; they are willing to take off-farm jobs; and many still identify with traditional female roles. Wilma Powell of Plains, Texas, would readily characterize her partnership with her husband, Bill, in this way.

Plains, Texas, lies just 15 miles inside the Texas–New Mexico border and is an about equal distance from Lubbock to the northeast and Roswell to the west. Like its simple name, this small west Texas town is flat, dry, and dusty. According to one of its residents, Wilma Luna Powell, "We're just lookin' and prayin' for rain most of the time . . . but we love it and we think, 'Well, surely it's goin' to rain tomorrow.'"[24] Wilma was born on the Luna family cattle ranch a mile south and a mile east of Plains in December 1914. She described her mother, Lillian Luna, as a "strong lady and a ranch lady. She just helped daddy when . . . I can remember when she rode horses and helped with the branding and everything. Of course, a lady has to help with the branding and cook[ing] and all of that too, you know." Wilma started helping her dad at a very young age because

I had two sisters and I was the boy. I had to be daddy's boy. . . . And so I had to do, well, I had to help daddy work cattle and we had lots of country here; lots of the country in and around Plains was leased. He had leased [ranch land] and we had 1,500 head of mother cows that we were pasturing for the Lazy S. . . . We'd brand and then we had to check for the screwworms. The worms would get in the brands and horns where you dehorn and daddy—that's where I learned to rope—'cause daddy let me rope. And if I missed it three times, then that was it. He would take over.

Powell had strong role models in both her parents. She learned both inside and outside ranch skills and used them all in her lifetime. After

Aerial view of the Powell Ranch, Plains, Texas, 1997. Courtesy of Wilma Powell.

high school and a short stint at a business college in Lubbock, she married Bill Powell in 1934. When I asked her why she hadn't completed the business degree, she said she was tired of school, thought it wasn't important and that "Bill was more important." The couple leased land west of Plains and gradually built up a cattle herd. "We started with fifty head of cows. Bill had about fifty head of cows and I had a few [cows] and some horses. And so that's what we started with and we just added to it." This was the beginning of a partnership that lasted five decades, until Bill's death from leukemia in 1985. Wilma spoke fondly of their life together. "We were good buddies. We were good friends besides sweethearts, and we had a real good life."

By 1960, the Powells were leasing ranches in two states and were actively farming both, nearly 200 miles apart. In addition to their land north and west of Plains, they leased the Alamo Ranch 30 miles north of Fort Sumner in east central New Mexico. There they raised cotton and feed for a feedlot where they fattened the cattle for a few years and then sent them to the sale ring. According to Wilma, once they had operations in two locations, "we moved our skillet" to the Fort Sumner ranch and went back and forth for many years, keeping both ranches going.[25] That meant

Wilma and Bill Powell on their cattle ranch, Ft. Sumner, New Mexico, 1968. Courtesy of Wilma Powell.

twice-a-week trips between their operations, but she said, "We made it work ... and we kept the farms going 'cause we had somebody down here on the farm, farming for us." Here she is referring to their hired hand, a Mexican man who worked for them for many years. In 1966, her father died, so she and Bill bought the cattle and leased the ranch from her mother and continued their commute for a few more years. Their burden eased a bit when their younger son, Ty, graduated from college and married in 1972; he and his wife, Linda, then moved to the ranch at Plains, cutting Wilma and Bill's travel time to one trip a week.

Wilma spoke of the hardships that ranchers take for granted when one farms and ranches on the southwestern plains, and some risks one doesn't expect. "You have some knocks, but you have to kind of breeze 'em over, and accept 'em and go ahead. It's natural knocks, you know ... blows with weather and death, of our mother and father and my sister and [in 1985] Bill." Bill's death from leukemia was hard to accept. Wilma "feel[s] sure where he got the leukemia was spraying cattle with DDT. I'm sure, I feel sure that's how come he developed that. Because I'd seen his clothes wet ... when he'd spray, he'd be wet and not change till night, you know—take 'em off and take a bath." In the last year of his life he developed pneumonia easily and was hospitalized often; Wilma was at his side throughout, learning how to care for him at home, for which the nursing staff presented her with a certificate for "Superior Home Nursing Skills." She had lost her best friend and partner and was still living on the Alamo Ranch in New Mexico. When I asked how her life changed, she replied:

> I kept it goin' and just done great [speaking through tears]. I knew what to do and how to continue and I knew this was goin' to happen. So you just buckle up, and I kept the ranch goin' and one day I decided . . . well, I was on top of that windmill and . . . the wind was a blowin'. . . . And I thought, "I don't know what the hell I am doin' this for."

Wilma was 74.

So when she had a chance to sell the ranch, she did so in 1988; "In a few months, I decided to build down here, and come back and, come back home to Plains where I was born and raised. . . . And it's been good because Ty and Linda are so good to me." They include Wilma in day-to-day chores as well, which she loves. Recently, she told me, Ty called and said, "'Mom, come help me; we're weighing calves today.' So that was my job, too." As she had done with her husband, while the men weighed the calves, Wilma kept the figures. She is proud of her son and his wife and their commitment to staying on family land in this ranching community. "What we inherited joined our land that we had bought [earlier] . . . so it'll just always be in the family. And they are doing very good; Ty is a good rancher."

In an era when many children of ranch and farm families choose not to take over the family operation, when life away from agriculture appears far more exciting and lucrative, the Powells' two sons were typical of many families; one stayed in agriculture, the other one left the ranch. Both attended college, then Ty returned to the ranch while older brother Dallas chose to leave ranching and go into the insurance business; he lives in Longmont, Colorado, today. Wilma has four grandchildren and five great-grandchildren, and it seems none of them are interested in returning to the family ranch, although she holds out hope for one of the current teens who has shown a budding interest in the family business.

Wilma Powell on her horse, Stranger, 2000. Wilma was 85 when this photo was taken on the Luna Ranch in Plains, Texas. Courtesy of Wilma Powell.

Because farmwork and family activities are difficult to separate, women's outdoor work is often overlooked by policy makers. A study done in the Great Plains region during the early 1980s showed that farm women participated in more than half of the farm tasks performed on their operations and contributed at least one-third of the labor, more than 20 hours a week on average, to specific farm tasks. The author, Richard W. Rathge, notes that household chores such as childcare, laundry, and food preparation are no less important than fieldwork and animal management, yet only the most visible activities, the outside tasks, are recognized as farm labor. Rathge's study applies to western farmwives as well as those living on the Great Plains and helps explain why many spouses describe themselves as farm "helpers" rather than farmers.

Still, many agricultural women resisted full-time homemaker status. They saw themselves in partnership with their husbands and believed that outside farmwork, self-described as "helping out," brought more status and personal satisfaction, and demonstrated their importance to the family economy. When asked to describe their lives, they sound contradictory: they are not full-time fieldworkers nor are they full-time housewives, yet they have a strong sense of self and view their relationship with their spouse as a partnership. They continue to run errands, pick up machinery parts, shut off the water tank, or move sprinkler lines. By "helping out" in these ways, women are able to deny that they actually perform farmwork and can then claim that they are living up to the postwar domestic ideal of homemaker. Like her urban counterpart, the agricultural woman is reshaping her role in a changing agricultural economy.

One woman I interviewed in northern New Mexico, Felicia Thal, has quite a different agricultural background than any of the others I spoke with and yet was named Cattleman of the Year in that state in 1993.[26] At the same time, Felicia has lived a traditional gender-specific life as a wife, mother, and part-time student of history, following and supporting her physician husband in several locations as his reputation as a surgeon grew and he became prominent in the field of transplantations. How she became an award-winning rancher well known in New Mexico and beyond for raising Hereford cattle is a unique story that defies fixed gender expectations. According to her husband Alan, "Felicia never had to think about equal rights for women. She just assumed they had them."[27]

Born in 1930 to British-born parents in Durban, South Africa, Felicia attended the University of Cape Town, majoring in history. The day after her graduation, she married her childhood friend and sweetheart, Alan Thal; the next day, the newlyweds left for the United States, where Alan began an internship in pathology at Cornell University in New York City. There, Felicia began graduate studies at Columbia University, studying with some of the most prominent historians in the field of intellectual history. After a year and a half, Alan decided to forgo pathology for a residency in surgery at Johns Hopkins University; the couple then moved to Baltimore, and Felicia enrolled in a graduate program and continued her studies in intellectual history. When her husband's residency ended, the couple moved once again, to Minneapolis, where Alan became a prominent member on the faculty of the medical school at the University of Minnesota. During their ten years there, his skills and renown grew in the newly developing fields of open-heart surgery and organ transplants. Again, Felicia enrolled in graduate studies, never quite completing a doctoral program but continuing to enjoy the pursuit of history. She described those years and her role as wife and mother in this way:

I spent many years on a part-time basis, working in universities until the time I got into the cattle business, which was some years later. . . . I worked on those degrees but because I changed, I never completed [a formal degree]. I would decide to work on a certain thesis, and I would spend as long as it took me to complete the thesis, and then I would hand it in and I would get credit for the thesis; but I never did anything else after a while. I didn't comply with university regulations to take this many of that or this many of that. It really wasn't important at all because I was a housewife and later, of course, a mother and so on. I have three children; two of them were born when we were in Minnesota in those early years in the '50s and I devoted . . . My husband's career was the first thing, apart from family, and I devoted myself to that. He always had a pretty demanding schedule; we entertained a lot and all that sort of thing. He became chair of the department; he was the youngest chair of the department by 1960, and we moved quite a bit and all this sort of thing.

In other words, the Thals' married life resembled that of most postwar Americans (they had become U.S. citizens during the 1960s) in this era in which traditionally the husband was the wage earner and the wife the housewife and homemaker—agreed-upon gender roles, according to Felicia. Still she sought out and found other ways to enrich and maintain her intellectual needs without compromising her gender-defined daily existence.

So I never worried; I always wanted to stay with it [history] because I loved it and I was terribly interested in it and I loved to work in libraries and just study. I didn't like to teach; I did a little teaching but I wasn't particularly good at it. I was much more just sort of a loner in it; it gave me private time; it gave me intellectual stimulation and it taught me all kinds of things about the country in which I now live.

The Thals' gradual involvement with animals and agriculture came when they bought a home on the outskirts of Kansas City on approximately 4 acres that included a corral and small barn. Alan Thal had played polo growing up in South Africa and the family had raised national championship jumpers, so "he was just dying to ride again and have that." Their two older children were 12 and 14, and he wanted to buy a quarter horse for them and one for himself "because we had this corral in the back and a little barn and we could do it for the first time in our married life. So that's exactly what we did." Then when the 4 acres proved too small, Alan told her:

Felicia—it was always Felicia—you go out and see if you can find us some land. See, he was always totally involved in his profession and all of these other things were always left to me, whether it was to find a home, whether it was to do this, whether it was to do that. And I was totally used to it and I didn't think too much about it. So I went out looking to rent some land for our silly horses because we were living on the outskirts of the city, and I thought it's a cinch; there's a lot of open country around. No way. It was all development land, and they didn't want to lease or rent us a few acres for these horses. This was about 1966, '67, just shortly after we got there. And my mother died in '66 and I had some inheritance that came to me, to this country. So we decided to buy some land. Now we're not talking big bucks; we're talking small, small [unclear], and so we went out and we looked and finally we found 79 acres just about 10 miles from where our house was on the southern side of Kansas City and not too inconvenient to the hospital, and, of course, we were still living in the suburbs. And we bought that; well, we made the down payment, we had a note, we could afford to sort of pay that off. And we just loved it and put the horses out there. Then we found out the fences weren't any good; we hadn't thought about that because we didn't know anything about these things. And so we had to do some fence work and then Alan said to me, you know . . . he said, you know, there's something called a county agent and he said, you could go to somebody like that . . . go to a county agent—we were in Johnson County, a well-known county—and find out what he thinks we could do in terms of having some cattle on this place.

So I went to see the county agent in Olathe who took one look at me and thought, "Please, God, don't let me have to endure this," because with my accent, which was probably worse then, I mean that's almost thirty years ago, and I also was an urban person. I dressed elegantly, I had this kind of urban manner, and I went to see Tommy Hall [the agent] . . . who took one look at me and thought, "My God, I really don't want to have to deal with this."

The two later became very good friends, and eventually Hall shared his early impressions of the doctor's elegant wife who was so earnestly seeking his advice. The agent visited their property, and, because the family was not living on the place, he recommended they buy a few steers in the spring then sell them in the fall and not have to bother with wintering them over and all the work that entails. And she told me, "He didn't say, 'I can see you don't know anything about this.'" So the agent helped her find twenty Angus steers and "they were wild." More prone to being aggressive than other breeds, these cattle sometimes broke through the fences at night, and she began to get calls from the neighbors saying, "Your steers are out on the highway and you're liable." With Alan often gone, Felicia and her 13-year-old son, John, would try to round up the cattle. "It was hilarious; it was also ludicrous and I was terrified; I was absolutely terrified. Then a coyote would call and I nearly died. I mean, here I was out in the boondocks, in the sticks, with this little kid, you know, and grappling with things of which I knew naught." But they learned, self-taught, as she put it. Her husband participated on weekends and during vacations, but his time on the ranch was limited. Hence, Felicia's life as a ranch woman began. And, as she notes, her background was unlike any of the other traditional ranch women she came to know and admire over time, other women in my study such as Gretchen Sammis, Linda Davis, or Editha Bartley, her neighbors in northern New Mexico.

After a year or so, the family decided they didn't want to sell off their steers each fall because the children had named them and become attached to them. So in 1967, Alan suggested they contact the American Hereford Association, headquartered in Kansas City, who provided postcards for those interested in starting a herd. As Felicia tells it, the "naive Thals filled it out and sent it in. Sure enough, the field man from the American Hereford Association called us, and within a few months, we had bought fifteen registered cows and a bull." That started them off in the registered Hereford business with a permanent herd, and they soon became very involved and came to know other Angus breeders, locally and nationwide. Their lives changed enormously.

As a result, Felicia never went back to history. By 1970, they had purchased a larger ranch and built a large home; their third child had been born, "my caboose child"; and the nearest campus was 40 miles away. Her new activities became priority, although not without resistance.

> I rebelled against it initially; I said I don't want to do this. Why is this being done to me? Because it was a new world. I thought about going back into teaching . . . but it just never quite [came together]. . . . Then I worked briefly, just to get away from this rural life that was overtaking me. I worked briefly at Hall's, with Hallmark in Kansas City, selling fine jewelry, just to get away from the farm. I was groping around trying to find a way to do something else, but I still had this small child and so on. . . . Gradually, I got more and more embroiled in it [ranching].

Eventually, they bought a larger ranch, near Stanley, Kansas, and built a comfortable home there. Shortly after that, however, Felicia and her husband underwent a personal crisis. They were enjoying "the cattle thing" as a family when suddenly Alan decided they should "go ranching" full-time. He had become disillusioned with academic medicine despite his personal successes and his reputation as a well-known surgeon. Felicia responded, "Wait a minute. I don't think I can do that." He talked of getting out of medicine completely, although she believed it wasn't possible. "We went through a sort of personal-type crisis in our lives and I questioned many things, and I questioned our marriage and all that sort of thing." She told me that, married twenty-five years,

> it wasn't me; it wasn't me. I didn't want to do that. And it wasn't him in my view of him; because what I'd married was something different. He was a totally dedicated, terribly committed, terribly driven sort of person who wanted to succeed in this field more than anything in the world, and I'd worked alongside with him to see that he did that. Now he wanted to walk away from it, and I was supposed to do something that I really didn't want to do at all. And so, the question became whether we'd go on with our lives or not. And so I made the renewed commitment to go on with our lives. I had three

children and I had a husband that I'd literally grown up with, and the ties were deeper than the differences.

Felicia and Alan Thal's marital discord is not unusual among ranching families, or any other American family for that matter. Often married couples encounter a crisis and either compromise and work through it or divorce. Some of the women I spoke with suggested such troubled times in their marriages as well, often citing depression, both theirs and their husbands', usually due to financial and economic pressures. For this family, each partner accepted a compromise in order to preserve their marriage. Felicia agreed to full-time ranching, and Alan agreed to stay in medicine. To do this, they began to search for ranch property near a small town where he could continue to practice. "Let's find a place where they need a surgeon and we can also have a ranch," said Alan.[28]

After much searching in many western states—Wyoming, Oklahoma, western Kansas, Colorado, Nebraska—and asking others in the business, they settled in 1972 on a 5,000-acre ranch in Buena Vista, New Mexico, 30 miles southwest of Las Vegas. The local hospital was eager to hire a doctor of Alan's caliber; however, Felicia's first reaction was not promising.

> I was terrified of the isolation, intellectual and emotional, at first when I was here. This was a totally alien world. But I had to do it. I had to commit. . . . I'm a positive kind of person. I've always had the ability to adapt. I adapted again. I threw myself into it. I worked very, very hard. We had to make it work. We had expensive cattle, all registered. I learned to be tough, to swing with the boys, to be one of them.[29]

Tough and committed she is, thirty-plus years later. Felicia honed her ranch management skills while learning the business inside and out and continuing to raise a family. An outstanding organizer and skilled leader, she has been active in agricultural organizations at the local, state, and national levels. In 1992, she earned the New Mexico Cattle Growers' Association top honor when she was named Cattleman of the Year. During the 1990s, she played a central role in the establishment of the New Mexico Farm and Ranch Heritage Museum in Las Cruces. We will learn more about this cattlewoman's activism in chapter 5.

In an article in *Cowboys & Indians* magazine, Sharon Niederman describes Thal's daily routine: "Thal always gets up very early. She makes her calls and orders early, and before 7am, has spoken to her foreman and made the day's priorities. Fencing, wiring, haying, calving, mechanical servicing, equipment maintenance—these are all her decisions. The seasonal work—weaning, merchandising and all the economics—are hers to decide as well. 'Then, I may go play golf!' she says."[30]

3
"I Didn't Milk Cows; I Gave Piano Lessons"
Will Wage Work Save the Family Farm?

"I didn't milk cows; I gave piano lessons," said Lila Hill, a farmwife who lives on a 157-acre farm in Meridian, Idaho, west of Boise. Together she and her husband, Earl, operate a dairy farm, caring for about 100 head of cattle. When they married in 1968, they were clear on the division of labor on the farm. Earl was the farmer and worked outside, Lila the farmwife who worked inside, with the exception of the garden and yard. For over fifteen years, Lila gave music lessons to augment the family income, teaching as many as fifty students a week at one time. Then, in the early 1980s, Lila and Earl agreed that Lila would take a job off-farm, one that would produce increased income in a period of rising farm costs and falling dairy prices. To prepare herself for the job market, Lila enrolled in a computer course, then took a series of jobs serving as secretary for several area churches, a position she continues to hold today.[1]

Rural people have always produced income from a variety of sources, both men and women, reshaping gender roles as needed, as we saw in chapter 2. Lila Hill is typical of the many farmwives who recognize that their most important contribution to farming may be taking a job in town. Working off the farm to supplement the farm income is not a new development but has been taking place for several decades as American agriculture has undergone dramatic changes. Lila is one of several of my informants who have worked for wages as well as doing unpaid labor on the farm or ranch. Historically, men as well as women have taken jobs off-farm in order to be able to stay on the farm. When this occurs, the workload for women increases on the home place. Martha Ascuena's husband, George, of Mountain Home, Idaho, taught school for many years while continuing to farm east of town; Martha was left with caring for the animals, repairing fences, and doing other outside chores, along with housework and childcare, until her husband returned on the weekend. From the beginning of their marriage, Elizabeth Lloyd's husband did part-time work and later full-time work for wages while continuing to raise dairy cattle on their farms both in eastern Idaho and later in eastern Oregon. When a back injury in 1956 prevented him from returning to farmwork, Elizabeth went to work full-time for Ore-Ida Foods in 1957, and she continued at the potato processing plant until her retirement in 1986. Still, they continued to farm and to care for a family of seven children. Clarence worked the evening shift while Elizabeth worked nights, which allowed her to see the children off to school in the mornings and be there when they returned later in the day. Equally important, Elizabeth was able to maintain the role of mother and wife that was expected of farm women while contributing to the farm income.[2]

Lloyd is one of many women that fit historian Katherine Jellison's study of midwestern farmwives between 1913 and 1963.[3] Jellison found that white middle-class women taking jobs off-farm was a relatively new phenomenon in the 1950s, and it drew mixed responses. Editors at *Wallaces' Farmer*, a prominent farm publication, took the position that wage work was acceptable, but only as a temporary measure until the young couple could "establish themselves." By the mid-fifties, however, farm women of all ages were increasingly becoming permanent members of the small-town labor force in midwestern communities, as well as postwar consumers. How did their consumer habits compare to those of urban families? Much is known about the consumer habits of postwar urban families, less so about their rural counterparts.

Nationwide, American families were growing and spending; that is, family size increased dramatically as the soldiers returned home, and consumer spending increased to accommodate both larger families and larger appetites that postwar affluence encouraged. The postwar years saw large increases in discretionary spending power. Between 1947 and 1961, when the number of families rose 28 percent, national income increased over 60 percent, and the group with discretionary income (those with money for nonnecessities) doubled.[4] Rather than spending for personal luxury items, Americans bought for the home. In the five years after World War II, consumer spending increased 60 percent, but the amount spent on household furnishings and appliances rose 240 percent.[5] Between 1946 and 1950, consumers purchased 21.4 million automobiles, more than 20 million refrigerators, 5.5 million electric stoves, and 11.6 million television sets, a trend that continued into the 1950s.[6]

Many of these new items could be found in fast-growing suburban cities. Here, in a crabgrass-free, three-bedroom, two-bathroom ranch home, young families could raise their children in a nice neighborhood complete with cars, washing machines, refrigerators, television sets, and other appliances associated with "the good life." Yet farm families also desired, and in fact purchased, many of these same commodities—assuming, of course, they had electricity.[7] By 1954, 91.4 percent of rural families in the Mountain West (Montana, Idaho, Wyoming, Colorado, New Mexico, Arizona, Utah, and Nevada) and 96.7 percent in the Pacific West (Washington, Oregon, and California) had electric power.[8] As we will see, farm families were not without many of the new consumer items their city counterparts were enjoying.

Still, U.S. Department of Agriculture officials estimated in 1946 that only middle- to high-income farm families would benefit from increased farm incomes. In the Corn and Wheat Belts, which led all other areas of the country in increased farm incomes and wartime savings, only "farm families with the largest savings look[ed] forward to having the conveniences that [were] generally available in cities—central heat, automatic hot water, telephone, electricity, and an all-weather road to the door."[9] One study listed the appliances expected by middle-class rural families in this order: refrigerators, washing machines, irons, radios, deep freezer units, brooders, and churns. As it did for their urban counterparts, increased income gave farm women "the opportunity, as one woman put it, 'to get some of the things we've always wanted.'"[10]

How widespread was this pattern of consumerism in the West? Limited sources suggest that at least some farms and ranches shared in the bounty. Martha Ascuena, who, in the 1950s, lived on a 60-acre ranch south of Mountain Home, Idaho, felt very content with what she had, which included a refrigerator and a conventional washing machine. However, she lacked a dining room set, so her husband determined that they should have one, went to town, and purchased a set that Martha has loved ever since. When asked if she ever thought women in town had more things or better things than she did, Martha replied: "I never in my life wanted

In this 1959 Bell advertisement, only the view of a farmyard through the kitchen window reveals that this modern domestic scene is taking place in a farm home. Courtesy of Ayer Collection, Archives Center, National Museum of American History, Smithsonian Institution, Washington, D.C.

things anybody else had; that never bothered me one bit. They definitely lived better, there's no doubt about that. They dressed better, they went more, they did things that way, but that didn't bother me because I didn't miss it. And I think farm women of my time didn't miss it."[11]

According to Jellison's research in Illinois, 10 percent of that state's farm women were wage earners, most of them working as retail clerks, teachers, or factory workers. Although wages were low, women could still make more money at town jobs than they could by selling dressed chickens, cottage cheese, or eggs—the traditional types of farm women's economic activities. Nor did they expect to quit their town jobs soon, even when a 40-mile round-trip commute was part of the job. According to the *Wallaces' Farmer* editor, "It isn't for a TV set or a home freezer that Harriet Sellers, R.N. and homemaker, is spending her salary. It's for school clothing, groceries, tractor fuel and farm payments. . . . Practically speaking, it seems that mom has come to town so dad and the kids can stay on the farm."[12] Many western farm families fit this pattern as well, engaging in wage labor to supplement agricultural income.

Wage labor has often meant the difference between staying in agriculture and selling the family farm. It is one more form of diversification, providing income to supplement crops or animals. Lila Hill's in-home music studio and her later decision to take a job in town are examples of this form of diversification. Rosalie Romero of Chacón, New Mexico, counts wage labor as the key to her family's stability throughout their lifetime.[13] Linda Murgoitio of Meridian, Idaho, spent the first ten years of her married life working for an insurance company so the young couple could save enough capital to invest in land and equipment.[14] And the youngest farm woman in my sample, Terra Graf of Cortez, Colorado, at age 22, already has three part-time jobs in addition to raising cattle with her husband, father, and brother.[15]

Graf, who grew up around cattle and horses and rodeoed as a teenager, works at the local hospital one to two days a week, has her own business breaking horses for people who don't care to do it themselves, and, more recently, was appointed a state brand inspector. I asked Graf, one of the younger brand inspectors, if not the youngest, how this came about. She told me that since she was 10 years old, she has spent a lot of time in sale barns, learning about cattle and how to identify breeds. More recently she worked alongside an experienced inspector, who encouraged her to apply for the position. A year later, she is ready to test for a pay increase, "a good job to suffice [sic] my ranch part of life."

As noted earlier, farm husbands have long worked off-farm for wages. Graf's husband, Terrill, also born into a farm family in the Four Corners region, is a farmer and a welder. So is the husband of Terra's friend Marion Kelley. Both men have skills that are useful, if not necessary, for operating a farm or ranch and that they can also parlay into wage-earning incomes. Wage earners come in both genders.

Several of the older farm women interviewed for this study spoke of young women who work off-farm as a matter of fact rather than as a choice, like Graf. Helen Tiegs of Meridian, Idaho, described her daughter-in-law, who works for an insurance company, as "a good farmwife. She knows how to irrigate, how to do siphon tubes and everything" and is a "very good business gal" in addition to keeping the books for a local farm organization.[16]

In Martha Ascuena's view, "three-quarters of the girls are [working off-farm] because the farm just isn't enough to pay expenses. . . . I'm sure that income is taking care of the house expenses or even the groceries. It's certainly a different way of life."[17] Elizabeth Lloyd was even more direct, saying, "The farm was just a place to live really because even people today that have small farms—a lot of their living they get from outside work."[18]

Diane Josephy Peavey of Carey, Idaho, was one who did some "outside work," but not exactly in the order Lloyd or others have described. Peavey is representative of women who did not grow up in agriculture but came to it through marriage.[19] Peavey came to Idaho from Washington, D.C., in 1981 at the suggestion of then state senator John Peavey, a rancher in south central Idaho. A simple question, "Why don't you spend a summer on a ranch?" turned an urban career woman into a rancher (eventually). The couple married the next year, and John brought his bride home to his family cattle and sheep ranch, the Flat Top Sheep Ranch, 20-plus challenging miles off Highway 75 east of Sun Valley/Ketchum. Nestled in Muldoon Canyon, with vistas of the Pioneer Mountains to the west, lies "Peavey Country—250,000 acres of federal, state and private lands—consisting of meadows, foothills, sudden upthrusts of rugged volcanic rock and fishable streams."[20] John Peavey, a third-generation rancher with a son following him in the business, runs 2,500 beef cattle and about 4,500 ewes, which give birth to 5,000-plus lambs in the spring. Life was about to change drastically for the new Mrs. Peavey.

Diane was not unfamiliar with the West because she had spent many summers on family vacations in the region while her father, historian Alvin Josephy, gathered material for his work, especially his books on the Nez Perce tribe in west central Idaho. But, she told me, "even though I had all those experiences with my father, I had never really learned about that kind of remoteness or understood what I was getting into when I married and moved out here."

The ranch was an hour and a quarter drive from Ketchum, where John had long owned a condominium where he spent most of the winters. This small urban center soon became a home away from the ranch for Diane. She explained her life at that point:

> Even though I had lived in Alaska, I really was an urban person, and I
> needed coffee, and I needed books and I needed music and I needed

Bitterbrush
Country
Living on the Edge of the Land

D I A N E   J O S E P H Y   P E A V E Y

Cover of Diane Josephy Peavey's 2001 publication, *Bitterbrush Country*. Courtesy of Diane Josephy Peavey.

a lot of sort of urban trappings that made me feel comfortable. It [the ranch situation] was quite a shock and after I realized that I had gotten married and this was it, I looked around and thought, I can't, I don't know what to do. I really knew from the very beginning that I was not going to be the cowgirl of the year—roping, riding, and castrating everything in sight was not what I thought I had bought into.

Her husband was gentle with her, however, never telling her "she had to" do this or do that. He invited her to join him when he did ranch chores, and gradually she began to get a feel for this new way of life. "It really was a process for me of self-discovery. Or kind of coming to see the ranch through his eyes but not feeling like I had to suddenly become this extraordinary cowgirl."

As it happened, Diane had come to ranch life just as the farm depression of the 1980s went into its decade-long spiral. In response to this and to the fact that this urban person was struggling to learn a new role as a ranch woman, she soon took a job in Ketchum with the Idaho Resource Council (IRC).[21] She explains her decision this way:

Rather quickly, things started coming unraveled in rural America . . . there was quite a serious farm depression. . . . I took a job with a group called the IRC, which at that point was just starting out; I was the first director and it had just gotten money from Farm Aid, from Willie Nelson's concerts. I went to work and I tried to raise money. It was an amazing experience because mainly what we tried to do was reach out and reach the hearts and the souls of families who were terrified, who were in pain, who were suffering, who were splitting apart, who were losing their land, losing their livelihood, losing everything they identified with that gave them a sense of purpose and meaning in life.

IRC established a "hot line" that people could turn to for counseling, advice, support. She also traveled to Washington and testified before Congress about making changes in the farm policy "because that was at the crux of the matter." In the 1970s, the federal government and bankers had made borrowing easy; when "literally, the bankers had come to their houses, brought coolers of beer and pop and said, 'Let's sit down on the fence post and see how much money you need and I'll give it to you.'" Then market prices plummeted in the eighties, and those who had invested in more land and newer and larger pieces of farm equipment could not make their loan payments.

Diane spent two years with the IRC, spending the week in Ketchum and returning to the ranch on weekends. When she resigned her job and went to live on the ranch full-time, she pondered the experiences she had just had and how her interests might be shifting. She explained it this way:

> When I left to go home, I realized that we had been through a
> lot of what I'd seen other people go through, but we still had our
> place, we still had our family, and I suddenly realized what I had.
> Maybe I wasn't going to become that cowgirl extraordinaire, but I
> had this incredible place that I could now call home, and the one
> thing that maybe I should do was just write about it. . . . I wanted to
> remember because that same old saying that everybody talks about
> is so true—if you don't write your story, who will? And I didn't want
> anybody else writing the story for me. And even if nobody ever saw
> my story, I knew it was there.

She told me she stopped worrying about form, about style, and about whether she'd get anything published; she wanted to just write. She began by writing tiny stories, just a page or two, but they added up, and she wondered what to do with them. Then in the car one day on a town errand, she heard a woman reading stories on KBSU, the National Public Radio affiliate in Boise. She created a proposal, they accepted her idea, and she did five-minute weekly broadcasts for the next twenty years, from 1988 until 2008.[22] In the process, Peavey found she

> was able to open myself to the ranch, open myself to what was going
> on and look at the issues. I think for a long time, I hid from the
> issues. On our tenth wedding anniversary, we were talking about our
> life together, my husband and I, and he said, "Well, I just want you
> to know that these are the worst ten years of my life," and I said, "Ok,
> did I have anything to do with—" [when John interrupted], "No, no,

no, it's the ranch, it's the ranch." So I did really walk into a situation that was quite unique.

The Peavey ranch house dates back to 1890 and has been "rescued" and restored over the years. While it has been updated for the twenty-first century—they have a computer for e-mail and ranch business, a telephone, and a fax line—as late as 1960, the family depended on a hand-cranked telephone and an operator. But postwar consumerism was seeping into rural America, and soon farm homes were becoming more like urban homes. Katherine Jellison, in a study of midwestern family farms, describes the ways in which this process changed rural living forever.[23] By midcentury, the spread of both telephone and electric lines across the nation had allowed more Americans to participate in the rapidly increasing practice of consumerism. This meant that rural as well as urban homeowners purchased more vehicles, equipment, and domestic appliances. Since off-farm wage labor often accounted for these purchases, holding jobs in small cities and towns was one similarity between rural women and their urban sisters.[24]

According to Jellison, by the 1950s and 1960s, ads in farm-life publications directed at farm women differed little from the ads in mainstream women's magazines. Ads for home appliances were the same whether they appeared in the *Progressive Farmer* or *Redbook*. One image, however, that would not have appeared in prewar advertising was the farm woman as wage earner. According to Jellison's research, this American Telephone & Telegraph ad

> headlined "Farm Woman at the Switchboard," profiled Mrs. Clara Schindler, chief telephone operator in Perryville, Missouri. The ad featured photographs of the middle-aged Schindler at her switchboard and in her farmyard garden. The ad's copy referred to Schindler as "a farmer at heart [who] 'knows her onions' [in the garden] as well as at her telephone job." The advertising copy also stated that Schindler's understanding of the special concerns of farm people made her "the right person to have on hand" when a farm call registered on the switchboard. The copy went on to explain, "She's a farmer herself and knows what it's like to have grain that needs combining, or stock ready to truck to market."[25]

This AT&T ad featured a farm woman in her new postwar role as a wage earner. The ad copy stressed her agricultural knowledge and skills while portraying her as a new and functioning member of the corporate capitalist economy. Other ads followed that continued to minimize the difference between farm and nonfarm women's lives. One 1958 AT&T ad urged farm families to install more than one phone in their homes, particularly in the farm kitchen, where it "is so convenient when you need that 'telephone break' from your household chores."[26] While such ads continued to portray farm women in settings not so different from urban women, the underlying message reinforced the domestic ideology of the era that depicted farm women in their kitchens. In fact, that farm woman was more likely to be either working outside the kitchen in the farm fields or working in town for a wage. Such was the situation of Rosalie Romero, farmwife in northern New Mexico.

In cash-poor Mora County in northeastern New Mexico, small family farms dot the high-mountain countryside. Mora, 30 miles north of Las Vegas, is the largest town in the valley at 800 people. Many smaller villages, where some of my informants live, bring the valley population to just over 5,000. In 1970, nearly 60 percent of the residents here lived below what the federal government officially defined as the poverty level; nationally less than 11 percent fit that category.[27] Most of the families are descendants of early Hispanic settlers who came into the valley in the eighteenth century to create outpost settlements for the Spanish Crown. The families established numerous villages, enclosed by thick adobe walls, to protect against the various Native American tribes who considered northern New Mexico their homelands.

Before the industrial age made its appearance in this region, family members hunted, trapped, fished, farmed, harvested, sewed, and otherwise produced the goods needed to survive in the high, mountainous climate with short growing seasons. Typical of agrarian communities where cash is in short supply, the people bartered and shared goods and services. Well into the twentieth century, the Mora Valley remained a difficult place to live, work, and raise families. Various kinds of labor, along with farming, were intrinsic to the inhabitants' survival.

Rosalie Romero of tiny Chacón, New Mexico, was 18 when she first went to work off-farm in the early 1950s as a cook at a nearby school, then at the local hospital in Las Vegas.[28] She was already a wife and mother, but the small, struggling family needed the wages. She worked for fifty cents an hour at the hospital but remembered that "we did a lot with it." Her mother-in-law kept her children while her husband worked his father's land. Gradually Rosalie and Alfonso took over the 800-acre farm, mostly sheep, and both continued to seek out wage labor to meet their modest expenses. The extra income, Rosalie recalled, helped buy "coffee, sugar, the basics."

During their marriage, Alfonso worked for the Forest Service for twelve years, until he became disabled at age 58, while Rosalie held a variety of minimum-wage jobs over her lifetime. In addition to her work as a cook and as a hospital aide, she worked as a maid, as a waitress, as a nutrition aide to the Mora County Agricultural Extension agent, in the Senior Citizen Center in Mora, and, until her retirement in May of 1995, as a school bus driver. For both husband and wife, off-farm wage labor has been central to their agricultural lifestyle.

Over homemade tortillas, red chile, and posole, another Mora Valley couple, Alice and Frank Trambley, related some of their forty-two years together.[29] Alice grew up on her family's farm 8 miles south of Mora. She met Frank while baling hay (with horses), married him at age 22, and settled into farm life. After three of their six children were born, the family moved into town, where they have resided since, although they continue to make daily trips to the farm. They raise cattle and hay on about 600 acres. Half the land is under irrigation; cattle graze the other half.

Like many other families in heavily Hispanic Mora Valley, this family has always had income from off-farm work. In the 1960s, the Trambleys opened a slaughterhouse in Mora, drawing on family labor. All the children went to work when they were small; the sons learned to cut meat at age 14. Alice divided her time between raising the children and working at the business. There were long days, especially in the fall when eighty head of cattle a week were slaughtered. For twenty-five years, she helped with the slaughter on Mondays and wrapped meat on Thursdays. Today, she is free of this task since one of the sons took over full management of the business in 1992. Her "free" labor, unaccounted for in census terms, helped this farm family to survive. Because the work of family members reduced labor costs, the slaughterhouse gave them a cushion, providing additional income without paid labor costs.

Twenty years ago, the family invested in another income-generating business, a small mobile-home park adjacent to their home in Mora.

Today they have space for thirty-three units; they own fifteen units and rent out the remaining spaces. Despite the discomfort of sometimes noisy, rowdy renters, the extra income has been important. Along with the slaughterhouse business, off-farm work has allowed this family to maintain their agricultural roots through difficult periods and in a challenging environment. Alice made it clear that "we can't make it without these sources of income." As a result, their children will inherit a working family farm, one that has been maintained by outside income. Two of the sons live nearby and are actively involved in the daily management of the cattle and hay operation. Yet they, too, live and work off-farm.

Alice Trambley's willingness to serve as a cheap source of labor is key to the survival of small farm families. Economists Cornelia Butler Flora and Jan L. Flora, in their 1988 study of agriculture and women's culture in the Great Plains, suggest three conditions that allow the family farm to survive in a society dominated by capitalist relations of production: (1) provision of a flexible labor force, (2) absorption of risk, and (3) heavy capital investment relative to the profit generated.[30] Women play key roles in each situation. Because agricultural production differs from industrial production as regards a flexible labor force, the family is the ideal basic production unit. As part of a flexible labor force, shaped by the cyclic nature of farming and dictates of weather, women and often children are available to "help out" at harvest or calving time, or to serve as the one to go for parts or supplies. Once the peak season has ebbed, women can then return to other agricultural and/or domestic tasks, as Alice and her children did after the fall slaughter.

Farm women take pride in "helping out" in this manner and have created a variety of cultural structures around the role of farmwife. Basic to agrarian ideology is the notion that "the family working in harmony as a production unit is the best possible way of life even though that unit may be defined by the male in the household."[31] Unlike the case in industry, management, labor, and capital are bound up in the agricultural enterprise—the family—so all in the family are expected to contribute to the whole to make it work. Alice Trambley, as well as her children, has been integral to this system, helping to mobilize needed labor at peak periods in the production cycle. At the same time, the demand for labor in "her sphere"—cooking, cleaning, childcare, laundry, and numerous other tasks associated with being a farmwife—continued.

Along with their role as part of a flexible labor force, women contribute to diversification in production. Historically, women have been actively involved in agricultural production, most often the production and sale of butter, cream, eggs, poultry, and vegetables. Dairying, poultry raising, and truck farming continued to be an integral part of all farm families' work up through the 1950s and 1960s.[32] Women, and often their children, sold their fresh products in the local marketplace and received cash in compensation. When insects attacked crops or drought occurred, profits from selling chickens or eggs or butter became essential to the family economic base. These diversified enterprises also allowed women to control one portion of family income while reducing risk for the farm operation as a whole.

In addition, women's patterns of consumption affect the welfare of the agricultural enterprise. Because the nature of farming is land-intensive, it requires a relatively large investment to reach the volume of production necessary to support a family.[33] Women's willingness to support investments in land and machinery before household improvement is an integral part of their commitment to agriculture. Sometimes that acceptance comes at the expense of continued inconvenience and disappointment. For Sylvia Ortega of Guadalupita, New Mexico, also in Mora County, supporting her husband's decision to buy land rather than install running water in their farm home proved to be an economically sound decision. As she describes it now, "We were buying land and I still didn't have running water. He'd buy more land and I'd complain and get mad, then I'd give in. . . . It was silly but at the time, I wanted running water. It was hard, all that work. But it has paid off. Which I'm glad . . . because otherwise we wouldn't have the land we have. . . . We did get the water eventually."[34] In the gendered sphere of decision making, the male-dominated nature of farming prevailed in her husband's decision to purchase land. Ultimately, they installed indoor plumbing. Although Sylvia was initially resistant, she eventually acquiesced to the larger use of land as capital for investment, an example of how many farmwives adapted to situations not of their choice.

As noted above, many husbands of my informants worked off-farm as did their wives, and some of them made careers of both wage work and farmwork. Barbara Jeffries and her husband, Ned, of Durango, Colorado, are one couple who wore several hats at the same time.[35] When this

Colorado-raised couple met and married while in college in 1958, Barbara was studying business skills and Ned was enrolled in range management. By 1962, after the births of a daughter then a son, the family was living in Logan, Utah, where Ned earned his master's degree in range conservation and Barbara finished her business degree. When he decided he needed a PhD in the field they moved to Laramie, Wyoming, and Barbara enjoyed the two years there as a stay-at-home mom. When Ned took his first job in Bozeman, Montana, as a state extension specialist, Barbara applied to teach elementary school and was accepted. So began her second career, after mother, one in which she would remain for the next twenty-eight years.

It was in Bozeman that their agricultural roots began to tug on them. After two years, Barbara told me, "we decided that we were really getting old, and if we were ever to get a ranch, we needed to do it then because my husband was going to be 35 years old and that was over the hill!" So Ned resigned his position—"which no one could believe"—and the family moved to Durango in 1970. They bought a small place in southwest Colorado and rented land nearby from his family. They also purchased a real estate business, and in Barbara's words, "Since he was going into business, I knew we would starve, so I quickly applied for a job." She was promptly hired by the Bayfield School District and taught there until her retirement in 1998. According to Barbara, "We always laughed that really we had four jobs: he had a job [real estate], I had a job [teaching], we had the ranch [cattle], and we had the kids [family]." Together, their combined supplemental incomes allowed them to both survive and thrive on the several hundred acres they gradually acquired in the Florida River Valley northeast of Durango.

Wage work has been so prevalent for so many farmwives that Carol Inouye of Parma, Idaho, regrets that she never worked for a paycheck.[36] An active farmwife today on her family's prospering onion farm, Carol told me that

> in fact, that's probably one of my regrets, if I were to write an epitaph of some sort, that I have never really, truly worked for a wage.... During the high school years, I had done some of those field jobs like weeding, and I would get paid for that, but in those days, my check just went into the family coffers, just like any other farm labor

Sylvia Ortega's kitchen and the fruits of her labor in the summer of 1991, Guadalupita, New Mexico. Courtesy of Sylvia Ortega.

worker. I never did really want for anything; I went to school and drank all the milk and whatever anybody else did, but I didn't just cash that check in and spend it for my spending money, either.

Her husband, however, did work off-farm in their early married years. During the winter months he hauled lumber for the Boise Cascade outlet in Homedale, Idaho, while they farmed on salary for his father. Describing their financial situation at the time, Inouye told me, "We were extremely poor, I guess. I don't know what other word you could put on it. There were times when the children were very, very small, and we had to make the decision whether we were going to buy hamburger or shampoo, all those kinds of decisions."

Farm children almost always contributed their labor by virtue of growing up on the land, as Inouye speaks of above. And as noted in chapter 1, farm women agree in one voice that raising children on a farm or ranch is a good way to instill positive values. How do the children feel about rising early to milk cows, hoe weeds, slop hogs, or do the myriad other tasks required of farm folks? Since I didn't interview any of the children

Barbara Jeffries feeding her calves on her Lower Florida Valley ranch, Durango, Colorado, 2002. Courtesy of Barbara Jeffries.

of my informants, I can't speak for them; however, their mothers can and did. Elizabeth Lloyd told of taking her children to the fields with her when they were small; seven pairs of hands helped considerably as they grew to adulthood. Rosalie Romero recounted how her five children not only helped in the fields but also learned how to cook at a young age, saying "they helped me make tortillas and they loved to make donuts; they would double the recipe and make a bunch of donuts ready for when I came back [home]."[37] They also learned how to do the laundry, iron, and clean the floors, providing indoor labor as well. The Trambley family in New Mexico's Mora Valley could not have succeeded without the labor of their six children in several ways: in the field, in the slaughterhouse, and with the mobile-home units they owned. Overall, the farm family is most productive as an economic enterprise when all its members contribute their labor, paid as well as unpaid.

Life on a family farm in the twenty-first century is a challenge. Clearly, women do not make the choice to work off-farm in order to provide the family with luxury items. Instead, farmwives, and some husbands, work at wage labor to increase farm income because of the high costs associated with farming. Few farmwives today are disadvantaged by a lack of utilities (as their mothers and grandmothers were) or by an absence of laborsaving devices such as refrigerators, washing machines and dryers, home freezers, and radios or television sets. They have, like their urban counterparts, become "good consumers." Post–World War II accounts demonstrate that farmwives worked to pay bills, clothe their children, buy farm supplies, and generally support their families in ways similar to farmwives five decades later. These farm women take pride in and find satisfaction in wage work, which in turn brings them a measure of power within the patriarchal structure of agriculture.

In addition to off-farm wage work, some ranch and farm families have turned to another income source and one right underfoot: their land. The next chapter looks at various forms of agricultural tourism and how some of my informants have turned to both traditional (guided hunting) and new (bed-and-breakfast businesses) ways to supplement ranch income.

4

"We'd Be in Bad Shape if It Wasn't for Hunting"
Tourist Recreation on Western Farms and Ranches

Gretchen Sammis of Cimarron, New Mexico, author of the quote in this chapter's title, speaks for many westerners and their efforts to survive in the ranching industry today. For several decades, Sammis and others have found a supplemental source of income revenue in tourism. These economic ventures take many forms, some more extensive than others, such as the long-popular dude-ranching experience. In the latter half of the twentieth century, however, the rapid rise of agribusiness, among other factors, triggered a crisis for many western farm families. As a result, some turned to recreational tourism as a way to extend and sustain their agricultural lifestyle. For example, Peggy Monzingo opened a bed-and-breakfast establishment on her cattle ranch near Benson, Arizona. Editha and Bill Bartley provided guest-ranch services to families and children in northern New Mexico through the 1990s. Vicki Eld and her husband operate a long-running tourist activity, carrying visitors by horse and wagon to feed and view elk on their ranch property in Idaho. Other imaginative ventures include trail rides, cornfield mazes, birding tours, hay rides, "pick your own pumpkin" patches, and numerous other paying activities. This chapter visits with women who have turned to tourist recreation for a variety of reasons: as a way to make their own living as widows; as a way to diversify their family holdings; as an attempt to maintain their rural lifestyle and remain on the land; or simply by choice.

One of the most popular forms of tourist recreation, the dude ranch, has a long and colorful history in the American West.[1] Perhaps

Gretchen Sammis and her dog in the farmyard of the Chase Ranch, Cimarron, New Mexico, 1995. Courtesy of Gretchen Sammis.

unknowingly, President Theodore Roosevelt contributed to this form of the western recreational experience when he spent time in the Dakota Territory in the 1880s. Later he wrote up his colorful experiences in *Ranch Life and the Hunting-Trail,* published in 1899, triggering curiosity and a desire among easterners to "know the West."[2] Roosevelt had purchased a ranch on the Little Missouri River in 1882; in 1883, he sought solace there to recover from the deaths of both his wife and mother in the same twenty-four-hour period. For several months in each of the following three years, he lived the life of an ordinary rancher in what was then a wild and relatively undeveloped region. Dressed in typical western working wear—chaps, boots, bandana, and hat—he immersed himself in daily ranch work alongside that most enduring western figure, the cowboy.

Roosevelt's colorful adventures and glowing praise of the Dakota Badlands' landscape, the brilliant blue skies, and the mind-clearing business of the work at hand awakened those "back East," and the dude-ranch experience was born. Wealthy easterners began to think of the West as "a giant playground with horseback riding, camping, fishing, hunting, photography, wildlife watching, sightseeing and general relaxation for the young at heart."[3] Dude ranching proved also to be of benefit to ranchers, who discovered they could augment their ranch income by allowing "dudes" or "greenhorns" to come along for the ride during the summer season. Thereafter, the dude-ranch experience became a destination for eager tourists to "experience the West."

Tourism, however, was not born in the West but evolved as people discovered objects and sites—both man-made and natural—and, became curious about them. Likely the first tourist site was Plymouth Rock, known historically as the spot where the first Euro-Americans set foot in New England.[4] By the nineteenth century, railroad travel had become popular as well as prestigious, especially as railroads began to lay track into newly developing national parks. In *Calling This Place Home*, Joan Jensen notes that in the Midwest, as logging declined in the 1880s in central Wisconsin, logging camps were converted into resorts as a form of renewal for summer tourists as well as the local economy.[5] She uses the term "recreation landscapes," borrowed from geographer Timothy Bawden, to describe the myriad of tourist services that sprang up along the shores in the lakeland region, including steamship travel, hotels, boathouses, and dance halls.

Jensen also notes the impact of tourism on indigenous peoples of central Wisconsin, particularly the Lac du Flambeau band of Chippewa, the Menominee, and the Ho-Chunk. As the lumber economy declined, the native subsistence-based lifestyle was also curtailed as whites increasingly ignored native treaty rights to hunt, fish, and gather on Indian land. Drawing on traditional skills, native women and some men from these tribes made and sold curios, beadwork, baskets, and birchbark canoes. Indian men served as fishing guides; Indian women cooked and cleaned rooms in the resorts. The same pattern was developing in the West, particularly in the Southwest region. By the time the Santa Fe Chief was pulling into the Harvey House at the Alvarado Hotel in Albuquerque at the turn of the twentieth century, Native Americans had become an important component of the recreation landscape in the West.

According to western historian Earl Pomeroy, however, historians were late to explore the nature of tourism and how it has shaped western culture. In noting this deficiency, Pomeroy's work established a new field of study when he published *In Search of the Golden West* in 1957.[6] Half a century later, the study of western tourism is thriving. In 1996, the *Pacific*

Historical Review published a special issue on this topic. In her introduction, guest editor Susan Rhoades Neel notes the connection between tourism and cultural, social, economic, and environmental forces at work in transforming the West into an "American" place.[7] New western historians see the region as home to the most powerful of American myths and tourism as a most powerful tool with which to cultivate and shape the American experience. What world citizen is not aware of American cowboys and Indians? Of the Grand Canyon? Of the image of thousands of pioneers plodding across the plains to the mines of California or the green valleys of Oregon and places in between? The sense of "place," so central to individual and national identity, is thoroughly grounded in tourist sites west of the 98th meridian.

The late Hal Rothman, tourist historian par excellence, points out that the West uses tourism to enhance its economic, political, and cultural power. Entrepreneurs became skilled at producing tourist adventures that "created a form of economic endeavor that the West exported to the rest of the nation as traditional economies."[8] Hence the attraction of spending two weeks at a dude ranch where one can learn to ride and rope and round up cattle on the recreational landscape of the "Old West," or spend five days hunting trophy elk in the wilderness of a western mountain range. Early in the twenty-first century, "Home, home on the range" can be reinvented with just a little imagination and lots of capital.

Historically, Americans have considered wilderness in contrasting degrees of fear and appreciation. Initially, the earliest Americans saw wilderness as empty, barren space to be dominated and subdued. This perspective shifted in the nineteenth century when literary voices and artists began to write and paint the American landscape, particularly the western region, in subdued, rosy, romantic tones. They experienced and wrote of the wilderness as "sublime—a feeling of awe and fear at the transcendent power of God."[9] Quite in agreement, John Muir, naturalist and founder of the Sierra Club in 1892, fiercely claimed wilderness for its intrinsic value, commenting in 1898 that "the tendency nowadays to wander in the wilderness is delightful to see."[10] By the early twentieth century, the development and expansion of both the railroad and the automobile had created a demand for trips, tours, and packaged events. These experiences enabled tourists to believe they were partaking of the past, a past infused with and often wrapped in nostalgia. Perhaps the larger import, however, was the economic boon to an increasingly challenged American West, one in which the traditional extractive industries of ranching, mining, and logging plunged into decline after World War II. To offset this loss, many ranchers and farmers began to diversify their holdings to maximize their agricultural investments. By the latter part of the twentieth century, tourism had become the new "cash cow" of the West.[11]

Dude ranches are just one of numerous economic ventures ranchers and farmers have turned to as a way to maximize their income. One of the most popular and profitable forms of tourist recreation is the guided hunt. Hunting, once a requirement for survival in the process of settling the nation, has evolved into one of the most popular sports in America. Coupled with the increasing costs of making a living in agriculture, this popularity encourages many large landowners in the West to make their land available for guided hunts. In many western states, permits to shoot bear, wolves, mountain lion, elk, deer, or wildfowl bring in millions of dollars annually. And, as the title of this chapter suggests, hunting pays the bills. Other ranchers and farmers have joined the bed-and-breakfast trade; some have created businesses especially designed to draw tourists to their property for recreation such as a hayride and dinner, a sleigh ride to feed wildlife, moonlight trail rides on horseback, and bird-watching outings; more recently, they have cultivated intricate patterns in fields of corn, known as corn mazes or field mazes, to entice urbanites to their farm property around Halloween each year. This chapter explores some of these alternative forms of land use that often make the difference in survival of family farms and ranches.

Gretchen Sammis, fourth-generation heir to the historic Chase Ranch near Cimarron in northeastern New Mexico, has come to depend on recreational tourism since she opened her land to hunting in the early 1970s.[12] According to Gretchen, deer and elk hunting "pay a lot of the bills. The way cattle prices are right now, we'd be in bad shape if it wasn't for hunting." For the Sammis operation, "it's a secondary income as far as this ranch is concerned; not primary yet but it's pretty close to being as good." In allowing guided hunts, Gretchen has found a way to augment the ranch income and stay in the business she loves, raising Hereford cattle on 11,000 acres of piñon-studded mesas and canyons on the edge of the high plains in northeastern New Mexico.

When I visited the Chase Ranch on a warm October day in 1995, Gretchen and a couple of her dogs met me in the dusty driveway and ushered me into the kitchen of the 120-year-old adobe family home. She and her ranch manager of more than thirty years, Ruby Gobble, were just finishing lunch. The room looked as though her grandparents had just walked out the back door; a cowboy coffee pot sat on the back of the wood-burning stove, kerosene lamps lined a shelf on one wall, the round table was covered with oilcloth, and numerous ranching artifacts covered all the available wall space. Of course, she had running water, a refrigerator, and a modern electric range that stood next to the antique stove as well. Yet my first impression was one of stepping back into another era, a feeling that was reinforced later when she gave me a tour of the other rooms. All held period furniture, the walls covered with gilt-framed pictures of family members, the shelves full of rock specimens, arrowheads, Indian baskets, and other treasured items. A player piano and a baby grand piano, draped in a Gilded Age–style fringed silk scarf, dominated the formal parlor. Originally a four-room structure, the home now has a second floor, the bedrooms all containing massive carved beds, including the mahogany bedroom suite that her great-grandfather, Manley Chase, brought over the Santa Fe Trail by oxcart in 1867. Admiring this family treasure, Gretchen told me that "I was born in it, I sleep in it, and I expect I'll die in it."

A tall, handsome woman with short white hair framing a tanned and sun-lined face, Gretchen was born in 1925 to Fred Sammis and Margaret Chase, granddaughter of the original owner, Manley Chase. Her maternal grandmother, Zeta Chase, was an enterprising ranch woman who "ran a dairy and peddled the milk and the kids to school" while she drove the local school bus in the 1930s and 1940s. Gretchen's parents had little interest in staying on the ranch, but Gretchen loved it and learned ranch skills from her grandfather, Stanley Chase. She grew up on the ranch and attended the local Cimarron schools, then went to a community college in Altadena, California. While she was there, the Japanese bombed Pearl Harbor, and, on December 8, 1941, the students were taken down to the basement of one of the college buildings, where they listened to FDR's declaration of war "firsthand." After one more year at college, she decided to return to the ranch in New Mexico because she thought "there were just too many people in California" at that time. From 1946 to 1948, she attended the University of New Mexico; then she went to the University of Colorado, where she earned her bachelor's degree, then a master's in physical education in the early 1950s. Returning to Cimarron, she taught school, all grades including high school, until 1973. Even now, she says she still misses the students.

Raised by her grandparents, Gretchen began riding at age 3 and remembers her grandfather farming with a pair of Belgian horses. And she recalls gathering up and refilling the kerosene lamps, like those in her current kitchen, each evening, "like washing dishes and everything else [we did]." Finally, in 1940, local families formed a cooperative to bring electricity to the area, making kerosene lamps nearly obsolete. When her grandfather died in 1964, she took over management of the 11,000-acre ranch. She continued to both teach and ranch, doing the latter before and after school, but when she had to do it on her own, she made the switch to mechanized equipment. Today, Gretchen, Ruby, and hired hand Bill Doerr keep the ranch running. Speaking of her decision to leave teaching in 1973, she explained how the ranch came to her:

> My grandfather had set the ranch up in trust before he died in 1964, but no one but me really wanted it. I had a good teaching job which I thoroughly enjoyed, and I loved every one of my kids. But when the opportunity arose to take over the ranch, I took early retirement, and here I am. I believe that very early in life an individual sets priorities that he or she is hardly aware of. Deep down, I always knew I would someday be running the ranch and taking care of it.

She went on to say that her grandfather also told her, "if you really want it, we'll see that you get it, but it's like tying a stone around your neck." She really wanted it.

Although Gretchen never married—a fiancé died in WWII and a second prospect "didn't think this place was big enough"—for nearly forty years, she has had the help and support of her longtime friend and manager, Ruby Gobble. Ruby grew up during the Depression wanting only to rodeo, which she did for twelve years. She preferred to be outdoors with her dad, and he taught her to break horses, rope, and then trick-rope. At 19, she began roping professionally. In 1950, she went to her first all-girl rodeo and was a runner-up for Women's World Champion Calf Roper.

In 1951 and 1953, she won the Women's World Champion Team Tying, and in 1952, she won the Women's World Championship in Ribbon Roping. For her skills and courage, Ruby was inducted into the Cowgirl Hall of Fame, now in Fort Worth, in 1982. Gretchen, too, is in the Hall of Fame; she was inducted in 1986 for her efforts in preserving the historic heritage of Chase Ranch.

In the early 1960s, friends introduced the two women, and soon a partnership was born. Gretchen owned a good stud horse and Ruby owned several mares, so she made a proposal to Gretchen: "I needed a place to go with these mares and I said, 'Would you be interested in keeping these mares?' We'd share the colts. I guess my mares were here a couple years before I came."[13] Gretchen was still teaching and needed a ranch manager, so the deal was a good one for both women. Gretchen makes the daily decisions and continues to work the cattle; Ruby runs the heavy equipment and makes repairs. She is also an accomplished wood carver, and her studio is one of several adobe ranch buildings not far from the main house. According to *Hard Twist* author and photographer Barbara Van Cleve, "Ruby is a jack of all trades. She can shoe a horse, cut a calf, and artificially inseminate cows. 'I maintain the ditches, roads, and dams with the backhoe and 'dozer and do all the welding to repair the equipment. And I build gates and panels when they're needed.' She's a hand! And she can cook, too."[14]

Gretchen adds, "Nobody can do all the things Ruby can do." Although Ruby has some regrets that she did not attend college, Gretchen insists that "college is a good experience, but common sense is more important."[15] Together, the two women and their hired hand share the responsibilities and hardships of a lifestyle they all love.

The Chase Ranch is home to about 250 head of Hereford cattle. Hired hand Bill Doerr helps the women, earning Gretchen's praise. "Bill's a good hand . . . he doesn't have any problem taking orders from a woman. A lotta guys do. Bill's different—he came from New Jersey."[16] Describing the operation to me, she went on:

Right now, the ranch is a little over 11,000 acres, and we still run straight Hereford cattle. We also farm a little bit, irrigate a little bit, raise alfalfa and oats just for the animals, raise oats for the turkeys; we have lots of wild turkeys, deer, and we have one man that helps us, a hired man. [His] family lives right down there. He's awful good, he does a lot of things we used to do. I used to do all the irrigating and most of the farming and Ruby is really good with heavy equipment. . . . We still do all our own cattle work; we're on horse[back] a whole bunch. And we will be until the end of October.

About this time during the interview, we were distracted by what sounded like the garbled gobbling of wild birds outside in the farmyard. Gretchen got up from the table and motioned to me to join her at the window, to see several dozen wild turkeys pecking and chirping their way through the yard. "You know," she said, "in the wintertime there'll be about two hundred of them in the cottonwood tree, somewhere out there in the front yard; we hunt a few but not many." This comment led into a discussion of hunting on the ranch. She described the process this way:

It pays a lot of bills. The way prices are now, we'd be in bad shape if it wasn't for hunting. We lease it to the outfitter, and he worries about everything. If we wanted to worry about everything ourselves, we'd make more money, but what a hassle. No, it's a very lucrative business. See, this is mostly private land and a lot of available profit here. Hunting season starts the seventh [of October that year]. And there's some hunting up above us; they wine and dine these hunters . . . they're out to kill something. These guys are trophy hunters. They're paying big bucks to take a shot at an elk. . . . [The guides take the hunters out] for just five days, but it is five days for two months. It's Saturday, Sunday, Monday, Tuesday, Wednesday. Thursday and Friday, everybody catches up, and then it's time for the next five days and goes through the middle of December, then it starts again in two months. But there's lots of elk. We have a herd of thirty cows and calves, elk cows and calves; they get the best grazing they ever saw; they graze up here and then they come down here where it's fresher and then they go back.

Gretchen sees ranching and hunting as compatible operations based on her belief that "anything that grows has to be harvested; I don't care if it's grass, animals, or people; anything, if it grows, it has to be harvested; otherwise it falls apart." She speaks of a neighboring rancher who doesn't

Gretchen Sammis, Sandra Schackel, and Ruby Gobble at the Cowgirl Museum and Hall of Fame Awards Ceremony in Ft. Worth, Texas, 2002. Courtesy of Gretchen Sammis and Ruby Gobble.

believe in grazing cattle and also allowing elk hunting. She described his land: "Grass is this high, and it looks just great until you go through it and it's old dead grass and rotten weeds and there's nothing eating there [grazing] on the sides of the hill." She went on to speak of some ranchers who only raise game and make considerably more money than just running cattle, but "on the other hand, they're going to destroy, well not destroy it, but they don't get the balance [between grazing and growth]."

Like many of my informants, Gretchen has strong opinions on the role environmentalism and environmentalists play in today's world and takes an active role in local and national conservation organizations. When I asked her about the presence of antelope in the area, she told me, no,

> they are all out in the flats now. . . . Used to be they were only on one side of the road [between Springer and Cimarron], now they're on both sides. Just like everything else, everybody's after money or trophies, and so they don't harvest them correctly. They should kill a lot of doe antelope, but people don't need the meat; they want the trophy and they pay big bucks for trophies, just like elk. They don't want to shoot cow elk, but when push comes to shove and they pay

that much for a hunting license, they're going to end up taking a cow [elk]; but most of them want the big horns, to hang 'em on their wall or something.

My interview that day ended with a tour of the interior of the house; then we walked out onto the front porch, which faces east onto the family cemetery. There, perfectly still among the tilting tombstones, stood three deer, about 50 feet away. We all stared at one another a few moments, then one by one, they bounded over the old wrought iron fence and out among the golden chamisa. The rustling leaves of the large cottonwood trees, the smaller aspens, and the reddening sumac surrounded the historic adobe home with a late afternoon glow. All felt in balance that day, historic and timeless, reflective of the storied, and yes, romanticized, "land of enchantment."

South of the Chase Ranch and about 30 miles north of Las Vegas lies the small village of Rociada, at the end of County Road 106. Here, at the Gascón Ranch, I interviewed Editha Bartley a few days after I said goodbye to Gretchen and Ruby.[17] A friendly, forthright woman, Editha was eager to tell me her family history, which is closely intertwined with the small community of Valmora in the next valley. She was born in 1934 in Valmora, a tuberculosis sanatorium built by her maternal grandfather Brown in 1908.[18] A writer, a dreamer, a doctor (an ENT specialist) from England, William T. Brown came to New Mexico by train from the Midwest and built a sanatorium in 1904, then lost it. Shortly after that financial misstep, he located the available Valmora property, bought it in 1906, then lost it, also to bankruptcy. He returned to Chicago, built up funds, created a corporation, and returned to New Mexico where, as Editha tells it,

he bought the sanatorium right off the steps of the [Mora County] courthouse; started all over again and by 1920 had one of the best TB sanatoriums in the area, a huge, huge enterprise. Many doctors from Chicago came to see their patients—it was a Chicago thing—and, of course, they would come in the summer, and they always wanted to go camping. He loved to camp, so he would bring his camping gear; he had a bunch of good horses, of course, and they would camp. . . . The demand for a guest ranch was obvious because everybody that

Editha Bartley, Gascón Ranch, Rociada, New Mexico, 1995. Courtesy of Editha Bartley.

ever came out here wanted to stay, so my grandfather started the cabins, built the cabins here. People would stay, all meals were served in the house, and my mother continued the business in the summer, so I always spent summers up here and learned all the tricks of the trade.

Enjoying an idyllic childhood in many ways, Editha and her brother roamed the valleys and canyons on foot and horseback between Valmora and the Gascón Ranch. At the sanatorium, she explained, "my brother and I had to do everything; I refused to work in the kitchen there and obviously worked in the medical end of it. My brother refused to work in the medical end of it, and any time anybody didn't show up for work, we had to fill in." By the time her grandfather Brown died in 1935, her mother, Alice, had married one of the (recovered) sanitarium patients, Carl Gellenthien, and they inherited the guest ranch. Eventually they bought the 400-acre Gascón Ranch nearby, then continued to acquire parcels until the ranch reached its present size of 4,000 acres. They continued in the guest ranch business, advertising in the *Las Vegas Saturday Review*, and sharing all manner of experiences, "sometimes not too desirable, pulling calves and such." Editha believes that their guests learned that while ranching had its benefits, they really "didn't have it made in the shade."

Given her love for horses as a child, Editha decided she wanted to become a veterinarian, but her father "thought she would starve" in that profession and preferred she go to medical school. So after completing high school, she enrolled in Highlands University in Las Vegas for under-graduate work in the sciences. Then she met James Bartley, and her plans soon changed. Jim was seven years older, had served in the military, and had returned to run his family's dairy farm. They soon fell in love, and Editha set aside her medical school plans to marry once she finished her bachelor's degree. Today, when asked if she regrets giving up her dream, she says no; she is an EMT and "has practiced a lot of medicine without a license, I guess, especially veterinary medicine. Oh, I love medicine, of course, but I've never regretted that I did not go to medical school." But she does admit to saving old family medical books in case one of the grandchildren decides to go into the field of medicine.

After their marriage, they quickly started a family; their one daugh-ter and two sons were born at two-year intervals between 1955 and 1959. Each summer, she would take the children up to the mountains, and in 1962, the family decided to sell their home in Las Vegas and move perma-nently to the ranch. As she and her brother had done, Editha's children learned to do everything that needed to be done in the business of run-ning a ranch. "My bank president son is not much of a cook; he refused to work in the kitchen. Our daughter really is too small to shoe horses, but all three of them could do everything and had to. . . . They were all wranglers, dude wranglers." Their father was an accomplished electri-cian, plumber, and ironworker; his intricate iron gates, locks, and other metalwork are evident around the ranch today.

Raising a family and running a guest ranch require particular skills and are demanding jobs, not to mention that the latter includes the intrusion of strangers into the family's personal lives. Yet Editha never spoke of their guests in this way. In close partnership with her husband and children, she helped provide a warm, nurturing experience for their guests over the years, some of them returning many times. Knowing she preferred outside work to indoor domestic tasks, I asked how she had managed when the children were small. She laughed and told me that "I couldn't boil water when we were married but my mother said if I could read, I could cook. . . . I had to become a gourmet cook because we were selling it [as part of their guest ranch service]." Although cooking for two had been a challenge as a bride, she soon learned to cook for up to twenty guests a week, sometimes for as long as three months during the summers. "People with projects, you know; then we had sixty kids besides our own that we raised and that helped us in the summer, and a lot of them stayed with us a lot of times." These were children of their guests who wanted to stay on or who returned in successive summers, some of whom stayed for several months beyond summer. Editha credits Jim with being "gifted with kids," especially those who seemed like "perfect kids at home" but had troubles or issues that a few weeks or months of ranch work in the mountains of New Mexico often helped them overcome. She believes it was good for their children at the same time; now they have a "great corps of adopted-type family out there who are all good kids, successful; we hear from them a lot, they come back a lot. Well, this is another home."

The Gascón Ranch borders on the Carson National Forest, and because access was steep and took four hours on horseback, the Bartleys did not offer guided hunts. A stock pond on the ranch provided good fishing, and the guests had access to lots of camping and hiking in addition to staying in cabins on the property. The family continued to operate the guest ranch until the summer of 1989, the year her father, Dr. Carl Gellenthien, died. When he became ill in 1988, Editha took over management of her father's continuing medical practice at Valmora (the sanatorium had closed in 1973). This responsibility added a two-and-one-half-hour drive to her daily ranch activities. Her brother had had a stroke and was unavailable to assist her, so the family made the difficult decision to cease taking in guests after that summer season. In 1991, they held an auction, "the largest auction in northern New Mexico. Speaking about grand events, we sold over 10,000 items in three days."

Just days before the auction, however, Editha's husband, Jim, was diagnosed with a rapidly advancing form of Parkinson's disease. Her life pared down, she became his full-time caretaker, ending one chapter of their lives and beginning yet another. Because the two of them had developed an "incredible partnership" over forty years, Editha was prepared to take over the ranch management almost entirely. At the same time, she tried to keep him a part of the daily decision making. Each morning, she and son John would sit down with him for a "round table discussion," though eventually, Jim could no longer speak. Still, he was able to understand and agree with the decisions they suggested. Editha had spoken to me earlier of their partnership that had now become one-sided, with Editha taking on full management of the ranch with her son serving as a sounding board. After Jim died in 1993, the family spread some of his ashes in the mountains on their property, burying the rest in the family cemetery. Editha summed up her philosophy near the end of the interview: "Life is a challenge and it's always different, always interesting. But it's wonderful; you don't even have to carry money in your pocket . . . what are you going to buy around here? Don't have to think about all those things." And she added, "On the other hand, every morning is wonderful; it's a new day."

In *Dude Ranching: A Complete History,* Lawrence Borne notes the great importance of women in the industry.[19] Initially, women were central to the operation as managers or owners; when dude ranches became popular, women became frequent guests as well. A good business relationship between spouses, as owners/managers, and between them and employees is a key component to the success of a dude ranch. Because spouses will be working closely together, both people need to like what they do. Often it is the women who serve as hosts to guests, prepare food, raise gardens, manage any employees, and generally keep the operation running smoothly. On the wilderness side of the business are also women who serve as wranglers, trail guides, and packers. Women in these roles have chosen to cross gender boundaries in order to provide the western ranch experience to western tourists.

Bordering Canada in north central Washington state, the North Cascades Highway winds through a beautiful wilderness route that drops down into the Methow Valley and the historic town of Winthrop. In the 1970s, as the highway was nearing completion, the small community, formerly a mining, logging, and cattle town, transformed itself into a legally mandated western-themed town. Architectural guidelines control everything from a structure's design to the color of paint and style of the lettering on its business sign. Journalist turned folklorist Kristen M. McAndrews has written about Winthrop's transformation into a tourist-driven economy in *Wrangling Women: Humor and Gender in the American West.*[20] McAndrews wanted to understand the hardworking women who were an integral part of the town's iconic western images, those who work as horse trainers, veterinarians, dude-ranch owners and managers, cooks, packers, musicians, artisans, teachers, hotel employees, and office workers. In this male-dominated geographic and cultural domain, the women in Methow Valley use humor and storytelling to display authority and create their own professional and personal identities. As McAndrews learned, the women function successfully both in the wilderness and in the domestic realm. "These women can pack a mule, survive a horse wreck, cook up a campfire stew on tidbits, raise children, make a living, and tell stories about all of these experiences." The bottom line is that "tourists pay for a companion in the image of the cowboy dream— someone who will teach them about life in the American West, make jokes with them, and spend a little time with them."[21]

Although McAndrews is describing the dude-ranch experience, a tourist might encounter something similar in a western bed-and-breakfast establishment. Bed-and-breakfast operations have become a popular form of recreational tourism nationwide. They come in all varieties of sizes, types, and intentions, but all offer what might be called "the basics:" a home or cottage or room steeped in charm and perhaps history, a home-cooked breakfast included in the room rate, and innkeepers who provide both hospitality and food, from simple to gourmet. Because women have most often been associated with innkeeping, B&B operations fall into the domestic sphere, although many wife/husband couples manage such businesses also. Peggy Monzingo of Benson, Arizona, a friend of Editha Bartley in northern New Mexico, has taken the B&B experience a step further.[22] I've talked about Peggy in chapter 2, how she learned ranching as a young adult. One of her fond memories as a child was a visit to a dude ranch in Nevada when she was 9. Much later, as an experienced ranch woman who had become an activist on environmental and ranching issues, Monzingo decided to open a bed-and-breakfast as a way to reach out to people to inform them on these issues. When I asked her why she decided to do this, she told me:

> That came to be because I had time; I felt I could shift my focus from being one of the cowboys here. I had to stop riding because of my knees, [I] stopped being [of] physical help, and we decided that we could reach out. I had a list of a hundred and forty old school chums that I had put together when I went back to my fiftieth class reunions

in St. Louis and New York State. Using that as a base, I thought we could start communicating about these western issues that don't even get into the newspapers enough for people to know there's an issue, much less hear both sides of it. I decided that was something I could do, and my son went along with it. It's just sort of grown a little bit. I don't have wall-to-wall guests; I can't handle that because I do it all myself. We have had very interesting and good contacts with delightful people in the past four or five years.

Although Peggy sees her B&B as a way to inform her guests and, she hopes, encourage their support on western ranching issues, her guests make it clear they are attracted to the ranch experience, including the meals, and the reasonable cost. In her words, "We don't price our bed-and-breakfast very high because if I did, I'd have to use most of the income from it for help to keep it tidier." Nor does she belong to B&B associations because she doesn't "want to be overrun with reservations without feeling that I am in control of it." Many of her guests are repeat visitors, based on word-of-mouth recommendations, who make requests for some of her specialties such as biscuits and gravy for breakfast. While her suppers for the B&B guests are simple—bean burritos are a favorite—Peggy also holds large cookouts featuring a pit barbecue in which the beef cooks in the ground in burlap sacks. She keeps the accompaniments simple: "my frijoles, my home-made salsa and coleslaw with a special dressing, homemade rolls . . . homemade but simple, and people go absolutely bananas!" So, as she put it, "the cooking isn't hard, but I love it and I guess I've developed sort of a reputation." And typical of farm- and ranchwives, she always has the coffee pot on the stove. Whether they were hauling cattle or staging a roundup, she reflected, they "had doughnuts and homemade cakes and things for people to snack on . . . and we'd put on a meal at noon."

Peggy shared an anecdote with me about an incident that took her a while to live down. In her words, "I hate to admit, but the first roundup I cooked for, I cooked lamb stew! I have never been allowed to forget it." But sometimes her guests forget they are in beef country and ask for chicken.

That was close to Thanksgiving . . . and I said, "Now listen, we're in beef country." I said, "We do a wonderful pit barbecue and grilling steaks and I suppose I could grill some chicken." I said, "How about this? How about my putting a turkey in the pit with the beef since it's close to Thanksgiving?" So that's what we settled on. I assumed they would sort of eat one menu or the other, but everybody ate everything. It was wonderful.

Peggy has created a life for herself close to the land she came to love in her twenties through marriages to two husbands. Despite divorce and death, she has found ways to maintain her ranching lifestyle. Her keen interest in the political side of ranching, especially as regards the split between conservationists and environmentalists, has propelled her into an activist role. The bed-and-breakfast business helps carry the ranch expenditures and provides justification for her activist interests. In chapter 5, we will explore her passion for "shaping perspectives" around contemporary agricultural issues.

Opportunities for westerners to engage in tourist businesses are probably as varied as the type of land they own and their imagination. Dude ranches still draw a crowd. Just ask Patricia and Kim Chesser, who own and operate the 15,000-acre Burnt Well Ranch near Roswell, New Mexico. Patricia sums up the ranch's appeal this way: "Every American boy, when he's five, wants to grow up to be a cowboy. And we give people that dream."[23] Nowadays, of course, that dream includes girls and women, and folks of all ages take them up on their offer. The Chessers offer three week-long cattle drives annually and often welcome back repeat visitors. The guests round up cattle for branding, move them from pasture to pasture, sleep on cowboy bedrolls (mattresses and blankets enclosed in canvas) in cowboy teepees—simple canvas tents hung from two crossed poles. And they eat. Patricia serves up family-style meals at her kitchen table in the ranch house featuring "Dutch-oven wonders from the campfire."

You are advised to bring boots, but if you don't arrive with a cowboy hat, you can choose one from the Chessers' hat-rack collection. "Everyone looks good in a cowboy hat," says guest and photographer Chuck West. Slickers are provided for the occasional New Mexico summer shower. Irish American author David Moore described the scene: "Hunkered down under our hats, our scarves covering most of our faces, we look like bandits as we head across the plains. At the end of the day, we gather around the fire, trying to stamp feeling back into our feet, clutching our coffee cups with both hands for warmth, and commiserate."[24]

Gail Doran moves cattle at the Piñon Cattle Company, a working ranch and guest ranch in Weed, New Mexico, 1999. Courtesy of Chuck West Photography, Santa Fe, New Mexico.

Like many other westerners, the Chessers operate the dude ranch to supplement their ranching income, but the guests take away a great deal themselves. Far removed from their normal daily routines, guests are free to reflect on anything and nothing. Out on the plains among a sea of black Angus-cross cattle, there's time to spend with yourself in a way that's refreshing and profound in a simplistic, meditative way. And there are things you can't do at the Burnt Well Ranch—watch TV, access the Internet, enjoy a spa treatment or any other luxury activity available at resorts. Patricia explains why: "We want the guests to slow down, and spend time with each other. People call and ask what activities we offer for their children. I tell them we don't have anything special, except a safe environment they can run around and get dirty in. Some of them are suspicious at first, but after a few days they start to understand."[25]

This isn't a resort hotel with a few horses thrown in but a family-owned working ranch, a threatened way of life as family ranches continue to decline. The Chessers started taking in guests in 2003; "[C]ows don't pay the bills any more," says Kim. As more ranches and farms continue to disappear then reappear as subdivisions or are bought by large corporations, families like the Chessers provide a niche that visitors are willing to fill, to the advantage of both groups. What could be more satisfying than closing the day with an iconic American scene: the silhouetted figures of cattle and cowhands drifting into a southwestern sunset?

Eilene and Clint Evans, ranchers in Garden Valley, Idaho, an hour's drive north of Boise, have found an alternative to the traditional western cattle operation and now raise elk on their former cattle ranch. Elk Springs Ranch is located at the eastern edge of the Boise National Forest along the Middlefork of the Salmon, a popular rafting and kayaking stretch of the Payette River. Green rolling hills and clear spring water provide a natural habitat for their herd of 100 bulls and cow elk. Eilene and Clint Evans both grew up on farms in Utah and are no strangers to raising animals. Clint, a chemical engineer, and Eilene, a teacher, both retired now, have "always had a ranch in their lives" while raising children and also working off-ranch for wages. Eilene echoed many other mothers in this study who spoke to the value and importance of hard work that the agricultural lifestyle instills in children. They raised four sons and one daughter on ranches, primarily in Idaho, and although none of the children returned after college, they reassure their parents that they are "glad they grew up on a ranch."[26]

Like many others, this family has combined ranching with wage labor to sustain them economically. According to Eilene, no matter where they lived, Clint "always want[ed] a ranch," but his work as an engineer often took him away from the family, leaving Eilene and the children to carry out the daily chores. She also took care of the bookkeeping as well as teaching school. Every summer, the kids each raised a cow and learned what it means to work hard and care for animals. Gradually, they grew up and went off to college, and their parents grew older as well. Eilene said they decided to sell the cattle and raise elk for two reasons: because it is easier than raising cattle and because she and Clint are getting older; she is 68 and he is nearing 70.

They bought the Garden Valley ranch in 1989. Living and working in a rural setting is important to the Evanses. But, Eilene reminded me, "you have to be committed." Then, as agricultural conditions for ranching worsened in the 1980s, they were forced to make a change. Because they wanted to remain on the land, they began to research and consider raising domestic elk. Both of them told me that elk are easier to raise and more economical because "you can feed three elk to one cow." You do have to maintain high fences, however—8 to 9 feet—and labor to repair them. In 1991, the Evans made the switch to elk. Their original stock are descendants of elk that the federal government sold to private owners in the 1950s.[27] In the West, the animals came from Yellowstone National Park, where their population had increased beyond the carrying load, or what the land could support. The elk industry is heavily regulated in Idaho and by the Department of Agriculture at the federal level. Their ranch currently supports a herd of 100 purebred registered Rocky Mountain elk and is one of sixty elk ranches in Idaho.

A major part of their decision to raise elk included the opportunity to hold guided hunts each fall. They offer hunting in two locations, one a small, simple operation on their property, the other a resort lodge with amenities on the edge of the Salmon National Forest bordering the Continental Divide on Idaho's eastern border. The Evanses are partners with others in this venture, which consists of a 1,650-acre hunting preserve in the east-sloping foothills of the Lemhi Mountains. The accommodations there include a full-service lodge and several restored homestead cabins. They welcome nonhunting guests to fish their private trout ponds as well. This operation requires lots of labor, including cooks, housekeeping staff, ranch hands, and, of course, hunting guides. Back in Garden Valley, where Clint leads the hunts, the Evanses rent out one cabin on their property and provide the supplies and labor.

As part of the hunting experience, the Evanses offer numerous services. They arrange for harvested elk to be skinned, cleaned, cooled, and quartered, ready to carry out; or they will have the meat butchered, wrapped, and frozen locally, ready on departure or for shipping. They create gift packages as well for their clients. They also harvest antler velvet, a natural product that they then sell to a pharmaceutical company that freeze-dries the tissue, grinds it into a powder, and produces capsules. The ingredients in this product are said to promote energy, strengthen body systems, and improve bone and joint health, including arthritis. This form of alternative farming/ranching has allowed the Evanses to extend their ranching lifestyle and remain on the land even as they gradually reduce their elk herd. Looking ahead to their post-seventy years, they plan to replace the elk with a few cattle and ranch on a smaller scale. Their commitment to ranching has never wavered.

Verna Muncy, daughter of ranch manager Rick Muncy, drags a calf to the branding fire at the Piñon Cattle Company guest ranch, Weed, New Mexico, 1999. Courtesy of Chuck West Photography, Santa Fe, New Mexico.

In the early twenty-first century, even as the number of farms, ranches, and people who engage in agriculture continues to decrease, the power of their love for the land remains. Although many have given up and sold their property or passed it on to heirs, others have found alternative farming or ranching methods to sustain them economically in this lifestyle. One of the most productive arenas has proven to be in tourist recreation. According to Clint Evans, he and his wife, Eilene, have been able to "extend ranch life by diversifying" with guided elk hunts. In the twenty-first century, tourist recreation in the West has many faces and purposes. From guided hunts of both domesticated and wild animals to dude ranches and bed-and-breakfast operations, from hayrides to corn mazes, westerners have found ways to extend and expand their lifestyles and augment their incomes to allow them to maintain a cherished way of life. Peggy Monzingo put it in spiritual terms: "There is no doubt that what I am in is a very large and wonderful cathedral every day of my life." And from this western place, Peggy and other women expend time and energy on agricultural activism, the subject of chapter 5.

5

"Eat More Beef"

Ranch and Farm Women as Activists

"Nothing happens very fast," said Mabel Dobbs of the Quarter Circle Lazy S Ranch in southwestern Idaho."[1] Dobbs was speaking of the slow pace that characterizes activist causes, notably those in the agricultural industry, in which she has been active for more than twenty years. During my research, it quickly became clear that farm and ranch women, like American women nationwide, are no strangers to political activism and volunteerism.[2]

Women's participation in public organizing has a rich and well-documented history. The long struggle of American women to achieve female suffrage is one notable example; the reemergence of the women's movement in the late 1960s and early 1970s marks another period of intense political activism. Since then, ranch and farm women have been quick to add their voices to agricultural discussions on many levels.

Among my interviewees, Mabel Dobbs, Felicia Thal, Peggy Monzingo, Helen Tiegs, Editha Bartley, and Gretchen Sammis, as well as others, were among these voices. They spoke strongly about the need and desire "to give back to the community" to enhance the rural way of life. They find meaning in service to their local communities—serving on the school board, for example—along with attending soccer games, band concerts, and other family-centered activities. Efforts such as these are especially demanding in an era when more women than ever before are entering the labor market. Yet these women choose to engage in activities that require time, energy, leadership skills, and a willingness to engage beyond family, farm, and home.[3] Most of my subjects became involved at the local grassroots level before moving into more wide-ranging efforts at the state and/or national level. Yet, in this shifting and uncertain period in agriculture, women continue to devote time and energy to changing, improving, or expanding their rural way of life. In this chapter, you will hear from several farmers and ranchers how their passion for a cause marks them as women "who get things done."

First, a note about the myriad of agricultural organizations and associations that dot the farm landscape today. Like Franklin Roosevelt's "alphabet soup" New Deal programs, this industry is not without acronyms. They pepper farm speech and provide a shorthand for commonly discussed groups and issues. For example, Dobbs rattled off the following in one of our interviews; speaking of the WORC (Western Organization of Resource Councils), she noted the IRC (Idaho Rural Council) and ORA (Oregon Rural Action) and their counterparts, the NPRC (Northern Plains Resource Council) and the PRBRC (Powder River Basin Resource Council), as well as the DRA (Dakota Rural Action), the DRC (Dakota Resource Council), and the WCC (Western Colorado Congress). While these groups are regional (the West), many others are national, such as the National Cattlemen's Association (NCA), the Rancher's and Cattlemen's Action Legal Fund (R-CALF), and the Livestock Marketing Association (LMA). Then there are the Cowbelles, which in some states now call themselves the National Association of Cattle Women, and the Idaho Agri-Women, who are part of the national American Agri-Women.

Mabel Dobbs of Weiser, Idaho, a small community in southwestern Idaho, was a forty-year-old banker when she met and married rancher Grant Dobbs, or as she put it, "got into ranching and into rural issues. . . . It gets so in your blood—I would [have] never thought, had somebody told me, that I was to become so attached to the land in the middle of my life." Grant, from Soda Springs and Challis, Idaho, has been a working cowboy all his life; for Mabel, it was an abrupt change from a life spent indoors in the banking industry. But it's a lifestyle that Mabel quickly learned to love. Today she and Grant live on 200 acres of rolling ranch land along Mann Creek 85 miles northwest of Boise. There they raise and market naturally grown custom-fed beef, a niche market they have carved out in today's competitive cattle market. Like many other farm families, however, they are sustained by an outside income source as well, their Family Mortgage Agency in Caldwell, a 60-mile drive from their Quarter Circle Lazy S Ranch. The story of the "cowboy and the lady banker" is

Mabel Dobbs in her Caldwell, Idaho, office, Dobbs Family Mortgage Agency, 2002. Courtesy of Mabel Dobbs.

full of drama, including a four-year court battle they won but lost when they had to liquidate all their holdings at the time, and a house fire that destroyed their newly renovated home on Mann Creek in 2001. Mabel and Grant are survivors, however, and their life stories reflect their gritty strength and determination, both together and as individuals.

Although Dobbs grew up in rural Oklahoma, she was not a farm girl but a child of parents who moved often as her father followed construction jobs around the country. Just hopeful that their three children would graduate from high school, her parents were surprised but supportive when Mabel announced that she wanted to attend college after her graduation in 1960. Following a girlfriend to nearby Northeastern State College at Tahlequah, Oklahoma, she quickly secured a job in the campus library and began taking business courses. By that fall, her hometown boyfriend had joined her in Tahlequah; he was studying toward a degree in pharmacy. As often happens to youthful plans, they soon shifted when the teens decided to marry in November of that year. By the following summer, Mabel was pregnant with their first child, Kim. Yet just when her young husband decided he should stay out of school a year and work to support his family, larger events changed their lives once more.

Grant and Mabel Dobbs on their Quarter Circle Lazy S Ranch along Mann Creek, Weiser, Idaho, 2001. Courtesy of Grant and Mabel Dobbs.

In August of that year, the United States found itself toe-to-toe with the USSR over nuclear missiles based in Cuba. As Mabel told me, "The Cuban missile thing came up, so he decided—no, we decided—we'd better figure out how to keep him in school so he wouldn't get drafted." By this time, the couple had moved back to their hometown of Jay, Oklahoma. Mabel stayed out of college to have the baby that December, and Ron attended a small junior college nearby. As in other young college-bound families, then and now, Ron worked weekends, and their families helped with childcare. The next semester, Mabel "crammed all the business courses I could cram in, to where I had the equivalent, by summertime, of two years with summer school and everything." At that point, they knew they would be moving so Ron could attend pharmacy school, probably at the University of Oklahoma in Oklahoma City. Once again, family ties helped shape their future. Ron had an aunt in Albuquerque, who, Mabel said, he "wasn't even close to," but who had heard about his plans to attend pharmacy school. She contacted them and, in Mabel's words, said, "Well, you know, if you would come to Albuquerque, I would take care of the baby for you and it would be wonderful." Ron could attend the University of New Mexico College of Pharmacy. Mabel went on,

"So in June or late May of 1962, we moved lock, stock, and barrel with a '57 Ford, $300 in our pocket, no jobs, knowing nobody but his aunt, . . . and a 6-month-old baby who was cutting teeth and sick for the first time in her life."

They quickly rented an apartment, and Mabel applied for three jobs the second week they were there. Two of her applications were successful, and after some deliberation between insurance and banking, she took a job with Albuquerque Federal Savings and Loan. "I went to work for $250 a month, as a secretary for them. And I stayed with them seventeen years, and I worked my way up through the ranks and was the first woman branch manager that they had in their system." She had one break in this period when she quit to have her son in 1966. By then, her husband had finished pharmacy school and was offered a job in Farmington, a small city in the northwest corner of the state. As Mabel described that turning point,

the idea was, Ron was through college, I was going to quit, be
mom and stay home with the kids. So I quit, went ahead and quit
Albuquerque Federal. We went to Farmington; we looked at the job
up there and decided we didn't like it, and after about six to eight
weeks of being home and being full-time mom—by 8:00 o'clock
in the morning, I was so accustomed to doing everything in the
evenings and on the weekends, I mean I had that baby fed, bathed,
dressed and back in bed, and [was] setting there saying . . . you
know, I never watched TV, had no life outside the job, you know . . . I
wanted to go to work.

To Mabel's delight, her former manager called and offered her a job again. She had discovered, as many women do, that "I found that I thoroughly enjoyed the job and the career. And I found that I was very capable, I think, of taking care of my family and working, too." So the family stayed in Albuquerque, Ron and Mabel bought Nob Hill Drug on Central Avenue, and Mabel regained her footing on the corporate ladder.

At this point, Mabel's life could be described as a poster story in this era of choices, challenges, and realities that a renewed women's movement triggered for both women and men. Her success as a loan manager made her one of the top producers in her company, but that glass ceiling still caused her to bump her head. She also encountered the kind of subtle favoritism that accrues to men who learn teamwork and networking skills via sports, in this case the young basketball and football athletes graduating from the University of New Mexico and taking jobs with Albuquerque Federal. "They were sending them out to me to train. And yet they were hiring them at more money . . . and they were advancing up the corporate ladder. And they were hiring them out of college at more money than they were paying me and I was doing the training."

In 1970, when a consulting firm reviewed company policies and practices, Mabel and one other man proved to be the top two loan producers. She goes on: "They found that here was this woman that was way underpaid and way under-titled that was one of their top producers. So they had to do something." Within a year and a half, "when all the equal employment was beginning to roll to the surface," Mabel went from assistant manager to manager but was assigned to the smallest branch office. Within six months, she was still outproducing the men managers in that office, so she was moved to corporate headquarters and promoted to assistant vice president. When I asked her about discrimination she had encountered along the way, she had this to say:

> This is along about 1975 by then. So I'd gone through all this hurdle of having to prove myself. . . . The biggest thing that got in the way was a bunch of men who thought that women had one place—and that was on the teller line or behind a secretary's desk. And, yet, all of a sudden they had this little rowdy, rebel Okie that was doing a better job with the building contractors than most of them.

Mabel credits the new laws around equal pay and equal opportunity for opening up doors for her and a lot of younger women in this period.[4] She also spoke of her frustration that "by that time, there were a lot of really intelligent young women that were coming out of college, going to work for the bank, but just couldn't understand why, in two years, they couldn't be where I was at, when it had taken me at that point, fifteen years to get there." Unlike Mabel at that early period in her work life, these young women saw the possibilities but thought they should come much quicker; gradually, they would.

Back to that "poster story." At the time Mabel's professional life was soaring, her marriage was crumbling. Her husband worked long days at the pharmacy, 9 AM to 9 PM plus weekends, leaving very little time for the family. So Mabel "ended up trying to do a lot. . . . I did all of my housework and that kind of stuff in the evening so that I'd have the weekends to do things with the kids . . . if we went to the zoo, it was me and the kids; if we went somewhere, it was me and the kids." Admitting that the divorce "probably wasn't a surprise," she acknowledges that she was in denial: "I thought maybe if I stuck my head in the sand—and I worked harder at my job and I worked at being mom . . . " Voicing a familiar refrain, Mabel recalls her thoughts at the time: "I thought, you know, we were the perfect yuppie couple. You know, we had always had a nice home, summer cabin in southern Colorado, nice cars, two careers that were, in Albuquerque at that point and time, fine careers, three great kids. . . . And yeah, jeez, [we've] just got the perfect life." Mabel sums it up this way: "So the '70s was a lot of exciting things and probably, you know, the job and the career and all that finally had happened was probably what pulled me through when the marriage began to crumble."

Mabel and Ron divorced in 1978; their oldest daughter, Kim, stayed with dad while the two younger children, Zane, a second grader, and Ron Junior, in sixth grade, remained with Mabel. A few months later, at the children's suggestion, she decided it was time for a change and the three of them decided to move to Las Vegas, Nevada, where her parents had moved in 1963. She quickly found a job with Frontier Savings there, which then arranged to move the family from Albuquerque to Las Vegas. Describing that move, Mabel told me that the recognition that Frontier Savings was making an investment in her career validated her belief in herself and her career choice.

However, while it was nice being close to family, Mabel really didn't like living in Las Vegas; in fact, she "hated the heat in Nevada." A vacation trip to Stanley, Idaho, in 1981 triggered one more move when Mabel decided, "Oh my God, this is heaven! I'm going to live in this country." So in June 1982, after four years in Las Vegas, Mabel, Zane, and Ron Junior moved to Salmon, Idaho, 115 miles northeast of the Stanley Basin. Her parents followed when her dad retired in 1983. This "hiccup in the road," as she called it, led her into the second and quite different half of her life.

As a small girl growing up in Oklahoma, she told me, "I always had this dream. This dream was, I was going to raise horses. . . . I was going to own a ranch and raise horses, but I was going to go to Wyoming and find this cowboy and this ranch and these horses." It didn't work out quite that way, she said, but "I did end up in Idaho with a rancher, a cattle rancher." It was in Salmon, Idaho, that Mabel met her cowboy, local rancher Grant Dobbs, who didn't own horses but had raised cattle in nearby Challis for thirty years. When he entered the savings and loan bank Mabel was managing in Salmon that day in 1984, Mabel believes, Grant probably wouldn't have done business with her if he had known, before he arrived, that she was a woman. But the bank president in Sun Valley had recommended he talk to Mabel Glenn at the Salmon branch. Mabel explained: "He doesn't hear well; he's an old pro-rodeo bull rider and he got horned in the ear, and so his hearing is not real good." She went on, "He didn't hear the Mabel; he heard the Glenn. And he came into the bank in Salmon looking for Glenn."

Dobbs was seeking a credit line for his cattle business. He had a cow/calf operation and raised his own calves but also bought calves and then fed them to yearling age and sold them as 800- to 900-pound yearlings the following year. Once his financial papers were in order—Mabel laughed and called it "the rancher financial statement in his head and ... on a brown paper bag"—they quickly developed a friendship and romance, which led to their marriage in August of that same year. Mabel gave up her banking job in Salmon and moved onto the ranch in Challis, and that's when her conversion to a ranch woman began.

Dobbs had grown up on the southeastern Idaho-Utah border on a ranch, earned his pro-rodeo card in the late 1940s, and rodeoed professionally until 1957, when he broke his back at the Pendleton Round-Up in Pendleton, Oregon, effectively ending his career. Shortly after that, his parents sold the family ranch in Soda Springs and bought another in Challis; Grant used his rodeo earnings of $40,000 to stock the ranch and went into business with his parents. According to Mabel, "Supposedly they come [sic] to Challis because it was a better, a milder climate than Soda Springs. After I married him and spent a winter [there], I wasn't sure where they got that idea." She described the region for me:

It's wonderful summer country up there; the feed is really strong, it's good grass country in the summertime, but it takes such a phenomenal amount of feed to feed cattle in the wintertime up there, because when winter sets in, winter's there. And it's there sometimes until April. So we started looking . . . immediately when he and I got married. We found winter pasture for our calves in California. So we bought a semitruck and started trucking our own calves and what he bought down to the Bakersfield area in the wintertime rather than feed 'em at home.[5]

In their first year on the ranch, Grant purchased a red roan quarter horse for Mabel, then bought her a new saddle on their first anniversary in August 1985. And, said Mabel, this is when "he set about making a cowgirl out of a banker."

For nearly five years, they trucked 800 to 900 calves to California each year, bringing them back to Idaho in the summertime and continuing to look for a ranch in a milder climate where they could keep the cattle year round. Finally, in 1986, they bought a ranch in Grass Valley, about 90 miles south and west of Elko, and an additional 400 head of cows. As Mabel described it, a generator provided electricity, and the phone system was a sixty-year-old toll station line threaded through trees and connected to an operator in Reno. "You might get out and you might not. And we were . . . one ring and the neighbor down the road about 5 miles was a different ring." Leaving a nephew behind to run the Challis ranch, Grant and Mabel

ran close to a thousand head of cows with just me and him and no hired help . . . and that's when all of the problems then began. The cattle market went to hell in 1986 [after] we had just expanded the cow herd. The banker reneged on some commitment letters that he had written to the Farm Home Administration for us to finance what he [Grant] had done. And then we ended up four years in court, fighting to save the ranches.[6]

And this is when Mabel became an activist because

I realized when we began to have the problems and went to looking for even information out there, there was no place in the mid to late '80s for farmers and ranchers to go to find help to do anything. To find out how to help themselves out of the messes and the Ag credit dilemma. They had always totally been so—they so totally trusted their lenders and their bankers. I mean, their bankers, they thought, had been their friends. All of a sudden, you have farmers and ranchers who are losing farms and ranches that have been in their families for hundreds of years. [This is the crisis], the '80s crisis. So all of a sudden, I wake up and I'm a rancher's wife—I've been a banker twenty years and [now] I'm a rancher's wife—and I don't know where to even go to look for information, to try and help us get through the agricultural credit crisis we were in.[7]

Their dilemma marks the period when Mabel became an activist for ranch and farm owners. For the couple personally, the dilemma resulted in four years of confusion, frustration, and expense that included filing for chapter 12 bankruptcy in the spring of 1987, then converting to a chapter 11 bankruptcy due to attorney error; facing a criminal trial on mistaken charges of cattle rustling when moving their cattle herd from Nevada to Oregon; spending over $100,000 in attorney fees; and losing the two ranches. They faced another jury trial in Malheur County, Oregon, for moving a load of their cattle from Brogan, Oregon, to a sale barn in Caldwell, Idaho, without an Oregon brand inspection. At one point, Mabel took a job as a waitress at a nearby truck stop just to buy groceries. Oddly enough, she found working a 3–11 PM minimum-wage job "a relief from all the court stuff. I'd go to work and for eight hours not think about any of the problems on the ranch. I'd walk out at 11 PM with $25–40 in my pocket from tips, which were a lifesaver to us." Finally, they had had enough, or as Mabel said, "We just decided that we couldn't do this anymore. It was . . . four years that we'd been fighting and already [it had] aged us twenty years. And it just wasn't worth the fight anymore."

They made the tough decision to sell the rest of their herd, and Mabel found a job in Boise with the Idaho Housing Agency as their senior loan underwriter. With a paycheck and benefits that could provide a living, Grant and Mabel began to face the reality that even though they had won in court, they were broke and tired. It was time to disperse the herd and start again, at 48 and 58 years old. Forced to pay $92,000 in bank attorney fees and over $40,000 of their own attorney fees over three years, they were so restricted that they felt they could not continue to run the ranch. They sold the cows and paid the bank, and Grant slipped into a depression. Mabel told me that that was "probably the saddest day that we had lived through to that point, was watching them load the cattle on the truck, to haul 'em away."

The next year, 1991, was challenging for the banker and the cowboy. They soon leased a ranch on Mann's Creek near Weiser, and Grant decided to put up hay to sell; Mabel spent most of the week in Boise, returning to the ranch on weekends to be greeted by an angry and resentful Grant. "I mean, he'd worked so hard all of his life and all of a sudden, you know, he had 'nothin' and he was, at that point in time, 58 years old. Too old, as he said, to start again, to work as hard as he had worked all of his life." In the next few years, as Grant slowly came to terms with his anger and resentment, Mabel gradually worked her way back into the mortgage business. Ten years later, in 2001, and in partnership with her daughter Kim, they opened Family Mortgage in Caldwell, Idaho, 25 miles west of Boise and 60 miles east of the Weiser ranch. After many years of uncertainty and suffering, Mabel and Grant settled into a more relaxed and peaceful lifestyle.

By this time, the Dobbses were living on yet another leased property in the Weiser area, and Grant had purchased a few head of cattle to feed the leftover hay to each year. This action brought Mabel's younger daughter, Zane, into this story, saying, "Well, if you're going to buy cows, I want to get in the cow business with you." At this time, Zane and her husband, Marshall Davis, were managing 15,000 acres in Paradise Valley, Nevada, near Winnemucca. Their interest in the Dobbses' next venture brought yet more family members into the fold; Zane and Marshall now live and work in both Idaho and Nevada. Together, the family decided they needed a niche market, something they could do besides raising calves and selling them at the sale barn. When a neighbor put his crossbred Texas Longhorns up for sale, they decided to go into the custom beef business.

Zane took the first step, researching the cattle online, where she discovered that the Texas Longhorn breed is very low in cholesterol content. She then created a brochure noting that the family does not use growth implants, chemicals, or spray on the hay or weeds and described their product as "basically about as all natural beef as you can get." Reported Grant, "The crossbred Longhorn has a sweeter taste to it and a great flavor."[8] Believing they could eventually sell twenty-five to thirty head a year, Grant bought ten the first year, custom fed them, finished them out in the last ninety days, had them butchered and wrapped, and they were in business, because "people want to know where their beef was raised and what it was fed," said Mabel.[9]

The next stop was to secure customers, and here Mabel drew on her contacts in the Idaho Rural Council, the group she had become active in shortly after becoming a ranchwife.[10] That and word-of-mouth have provided the niche market that now produces Dobbs Quarter Circle Lazy S custom-raised beef. From the sale of five Longhorns that first year, the family sold forty in 2002. They also sell roping calves and have started a new venture called Mann Creek Cattle Company Bucking Bulls, in partnership with Mabel's sister, Jewell Creigh, and her son, Tim Roberts, and their daughter Zane and her husband, Marshall Davis.

As an activist in agricultural issues, Mabel is like many other ranch and farm women in America. Unlike some, however, she has a strong determination to see change through and has not lost this drive, though, as she notes, "nothing happens very fast." She was past 40 when she came to ranching and rural issues, and says that

> it just gets in your blood. You know, I've talked to a lot of the young people that I've been involved with, with grassroots issues, and I said, "You know, that first forty years of my life I had no idea what was going on in the countryside." . . . I tried to look back and ask myself, "Well, why is that?" You know, I grew up in a rural part of the country, but Americans got away from really understanding agricultural issues. For so many years, farmers and ranchers were a very, very strong political voice in this country up until after WWII. . . . And it's kind of like after the war, we just all drifted away.

When I asked Mabel about her activism, she said that although she had always voted, she was never politically involved in elections. But in the mid to late 1980s, when agriculture was changing rapidly, she joined the Idaho Rural Council, and she has served in nearly all the elected positions since. Then she became involved in the Western Organization of Resource Councils (WORC), a seven-state group based in Billings, Montana, with over 10,000 members.[11] She described her satisfaction in grassroots activism this way:

The activism has brought into my life a whole new circle of friends, and the thing that's so positive about it is seeing young people like Frank James and Jeri Lynn Bakken out of South Dakota and a lot of these young organizers from North Dakota, South Dakota, and Wyoming . . . that are into rural issues. As I get older, it gives me confidence that there is an element [of younger people] . . . becom[ing] so involved.

She spoke of her children's and grandchildren's commitment to activism and noted that grassroots groups need to continually broaden their support base. "Well, you know," she told me, "if my kids can see this because of my involvement, maybe that's what it's going to take."

For his part, Grant dropped his membership in the National Cattlemen's Association in the 1970s because he no longer believed they represented cow-calf producers.[12] He was responding to the growth of agribusiness in this era, when the large packers were "taking control of what was supposed to be the producers' organization." Referring to her Oklahoma roots, Mabel told me that she has "watched what's going on back there with their water problems because of the corporate poultry contracts, and I watch what's going on with cattle ranchers in the West because of the corporate concentration in the livestock industry. And I'm saying, 'What have we got to do to get the American food-eating consumer to realize how important this issue [local food sources] is to them?'"

Mabel has spent the last eighteen years organizing at the local level to do just that, convince farmers and ranchers that there are many issues they can address if they will just find their voices. She has often testified at the Idaho state legislature and has traveled to Washington, D.C., numerous times to discuss agricultural issues "around the conference table with the Secretary of Agriculture personally."[13] She is enthusiastic about the newly organized Rancher's and Cattlemen's Action Legal Fund [R-CALF], based in Billings, Montana, which is poised to become the nation's new producer organization.[14] She said WORC and R-CALF "fought like hell on NAFTA" (and lost). They are now working on legislation "to get the beef checkoff done away with or made voluntary and directable" and to require country-of-origin labeling on meat.[15] The Livestock Marketing

Association (LMA), a trade group for the sale barn owners, filed suit against the USDA, arguing that the checkoff was unconstitutional.[16] In support, Mabel and others went door-to-door collecting signatures to call for a referendum on the beef checkoff. They successfully met their quota of 110,000, with 10,000 signatures to spare, only to have the USDA discredit enough signers to prevent the referendum.

In the meantime, the constitutionality of another product checkoff, mushrooms, was working its way through the courts and reached the Supreme Court in 2001, where it was ruled unconstitutional.[17] This encouraged the LMA members, and indeed, in June 2002, the appeals court judge in South Dakota agreed with the Supreme Court that checkoffs were unconstitutional. Despite the possibility of appeal, Mabel believed the judge's decision would stand. "So, you know, those two things we've worked on for the last six, eight years finally have come to fruition." She goes on, "I guess the thing that was probably most frustrating to me when I got into grassroots activism was the fact that nothing happens very fast, and particularly if it revolves anywhere around the political arena. . . . The next twenty years will be interesting, and yes, I'll probably be as active or more, as active as I've been the last twenty years."[18]

Mabel Glenn Dobbs has company on the activist side of agriculture. Several other women in this study described similar kinds of social activism that reflects their deeply rooted commitment to land issues. Not far from the Dobbses' Quarter Circle Lazy S Ranch is Helen Tiegs's row-crop farm in Nampa. In addition to calling herself "the hub of the wheel," Tiegs told me that she also keeps herself involved in Idaho Agri-Women, a national organization that works toward making the average person aware of agricultural issues.[19] As she put it, "Everyone is involved in agriculture; if you eat, you're involved in agriculture because I don't care what you eat, somebody grew it."[20] Their agenda extends to the statehouse as well, where Agri-Women "keep up on the legislation for the farmer whether it's for or against the farmer."

A broad-based organization, Agri-Women welcomes anyone interested in agriculture to join whether they own a family farm or work in agribusiness. For example, the current president of Tiegs's local chapter, not a farm woman, became involved as a result of working for the Pioneer Seed Company in Nampa. Although Tiegs "kind of steer[s] clear of the presidency," she has served as an officer and volunteers when the women

Helen Tiegs, a member of Idaho Agri-Women, with a display of "Seeds Grown in Idaho" at the Idaho State Capitol, Boise, 1987. Courtesy of Helen Tiegs.

staff a booth at the annual Canyon County Fair. She described one recent very successful event in which local Agri-Women prepared dinner for all the area farmers who do business with the local John Deere affiliate. The group is not large here in southwestern Idaho—active membership is about twenty. Tiegs explained that "it's hard to keep any kind of a large group because so many of them [farm women] work, so many of the young women work now." Yet I found that among the full-time farmers and ranchers, most of them engage in activism at some level.

Gretchen Sammis, owner of the Chase Family Ranch in Cimarron, New Mexico, is one who is active at local, state, and national levels.[21] Before she worked the ranch full time, she taught school in this small community in the northeast corner of the state and served on the school board for twelve years. She is a longtime member of the New Mexico Association of Conservation Districts, a public entity that dates back to the New Deal era when FDR created the Soil Conservation Service to help western lands recover from damaging effects of the Dust Bowl era.[22] This organization, in turn, elects five to seven representatives to the National Association of Conservation Districts, which meets three times a year in various locations. When I interviewed her in 1995, she was finishing out the last year of her second three-year term as director of the Southwest Region (Arizona, Colorado, Utah, and New Mexico). As the regional director, she was preparing to travel to Vermont for the national fall board meeting.

Gretchen was excited about the work of the conservation districts and urged me "to put that in your paper because we should be the primary environmental organization in the country."[23] With 47 districts in New Mexico and about 3,000 nationally, the organization has considerable clout with congressional members in Washington. They were involved with a name change from the Soil Conservation Service to the current name and work hard to inform ranchers and farmers on conservation measures.

Gretchen is also a member of the Cattlemen's Association, preferring this group to the Cattlewomen's Association, formerly known in many western states as the Cowbelles. Speaking of the 900 or more women who own their ranches or farms in New Mexico, she said, "Some of them belong to both of them [organizations], but I don't have time for both of them. I'm on the board of directors for the Cattlemen." When I asked her if she considers western ranchers to be politically powerful, she responded:

> No, we're not now. We're only one and a half percent, farmers and ranchers are only one and a half percent of all the population of the United States and we're powerful, but not like we used to be. Well, I'm trying to say when we get that many people after some things that affect so many people, it has a little bit of clout, but not like it used to be. But the thing people have to remember, and I keep saying this and one of these days maybe it will happen . . . but just suppose all of a sudden, all the trucks stopped running and nothing was delivered to the supermarket. Then where would the food come from? Nobody realizes that it has to come from someplace to get on the shelves.

Here, Sammis echoes Tiegs's worry about the distance between the source of food and its ultimate destination, the family table. As the nation continues to become less and less rural and more urban, the greater the disconnect between food and its origins. Then she repeated an anecdote she'd heard from a local ranch woman. "This is overheard, but a little girl said, 'Where does chocolate milk come from?' and the teacher says from brown cows." According to Sammis, this story is indicative of the need to educate the general populace about agricultural issues, an important topic on Cattlemen and Cowbelle agendas.

Editha Bartley, a neighbor and friend to Sammis, also finds a great deal of satisfaction in organizational work.[24] Bartley had always made time for volunteer work along with the family resort ranch because she "feels strongly about giving back to the community." She is active in the Mora County Planning and Zoning Commission; served on a state film commission under Governor Bruce King; is active in the Natural Resources Conservation Services; and is a member of the High Country Cowbelles based in nearby Las Vegas, New Mexico. She cut back on her community activities after her husband's death in 1993 but is gradually resuming her activist schedule.

It was through the Cowbelles that Bartley met her friend Peggy Monzingo. Monzingo had not lived in New Mexico very long when she was asked to serve as membership chair for the recently established women's organization. As she remembered it,

We started in 1961. . . . Bessie [friend and neighbor] was president
of the state Cowbelles and she appointed me her membership
chairman, which I thought, for crying out loud, I just moved to
the state; what could I do about membership? Of course, it fit in
the cattle industry here, too. I just started going around the state. I
took a map and I picked out locations of ranching areas and I made
contacts. . . . From there, it just grew, organizing I don't know how
many locals originally. But there was really the same things as now,
the same issues. We needed to get together, we needed to get the
word to the schools, we needed to get the word to Congress; let's get
together and do it. They joined in droves. I had a neighbor who lost
her son tragically to bone cancer; I gave her something to do. I said,
I need help and you know a lot of people. Let's see if we can invite
some ladies to coffee and cookies or something and see if they're
interested. Eighty-some joined in a matter of weeks.[25]

Later in the interview, Monzingo explained the origins of the Cow-belles in Arizona:

They're a group that was started in 1939 down here, five women, down by Douglas. Mattie Cahn and others got together socially. Ranches were very scattered, and in those days, you didn't just pop next door or run to Tucson, so it was isolated. But these were ranch women and they decided to get together once in a while and exchange news and help their husbands in one thing or another. It grew to a statewide thing and then to a nationwide group of 10,000 women; that's how big it was in its top day.

The women took the cowbell as their symbol; they thought it "catchy," and using a play on words, they added an "e" to "bell" to denote the female gender. In addition, they viewed the ringing of a bell historically as a call for the news, for example, bell ringers. Their monthly newsletter is still a regular feature for most chapters.

In 1986, however, the national group decided to change the name of the organization to National Association of Cattle Women. Bartley was one of the women who supported the name change; she also helped influence Monzingo to open her bed-and-breakfast business in Arizona after she returned to the state in 1984. Peggy described herself as always interested in land issues surrounding cattle raising. As early as the 1940s and 1950s, "when she was actively riding [in] the mountains," she was aware of enclosures, fenced-off areas created as a result of the 1934 Taylor Grazing Act, in an attempt to find out if cattle were harming the ecosystem.[26] She is clear about her position in the ongoing controversy between "the environmentalists" and the ranchers, saying:

We didn't use those words in those days, but were they damaging the country? So they had these enclosures that kept cattle out of an area and let deer and rabbits and things in that were the natural wildlife and already knew . . . it's there on the ground, you could see it. It did not help the country; it hurt the country and grasses, and forage inside the enclosures had deteriorated in comparison to the stuff outside of them. Of course, this is true today. We have known this all along and yet it has been the cornerstone, one of the cornerstones of this environmental movement that is destroying the West. All of their foundations of their arguments are false, one being that we are destroying the country, one being that we are welfare ranchers.

Peggy is passionate about her grassroots work to educate Americans on agricultural issues. She speaks strongly about the misinformation she believes has shaped environmental issues in the past fifteen years.

We have always been able to stay ahead with technology and new knowledge and so forth. We have improved these range resources that are not "croppable." You can't really do much with them except work with nature's framework, and we have improved them steadily since the turn of the century, by the Bureau of Land Management's own records. But you'd never know it from any of the publicity. All this has changed. All of a sudden, the BLM is not even recognizing that these people on the ground—who have cared for the resources for generations and they are sustainable-enough ranches, lots of ranches—are fourth and fifth generations of family on the same land; [it] can't be very badly destroyed. You've improved it every year; it's been steadily supporting one family. It is now supporting three and four generations of family.

This is the message that Monzingo wants to share with her B&B guests. And, she says, "I've been more successful in the last four or five years, since I've stopped riding and started the bed and breakfast to reach out to people. A lot more people are understanding it." Her guests no doubt arrive expecting a western recreational experience, but they leave with new knowledge of the issues around ranching and farming in the modern West. She is combining her business knowledge with her activist sensibilities to inform them

about these western issues that don't even get in the newspapers enough for people to know there's an issue, much less hear both sides of it. I decided that was something I could do, and my son went along with it. It's just sort of grown a little bit. I don't have wall-to-wall guests; I can't handle that because I do it all myself. We have had very interesting and good contacts with delightful people in the past four or five years.

Monzingo has been very effective at adapting her adopted lifestyle into a form that sustains her agricultural operation. She tapped into recreational tourism when she opened her bed-and-breakfast service and expanded her grassroots activist leanings to a "captive" audience through her business. At 74, she says that "it's a wonderful life" and she still has work to do.

Another activist ranch woman with a reputation is Felicia Thal, whom we met in chapter 2. When this South African transplant won the 1992 New Mexico Cattleman of the Year award, the awarding group, New Mexico Cattle Growers' Association (NMCGA), was well aware of Thal's abilities and talents. Appointed chair of the Research and Improvement Committee in 1978, she invited speakers from across the nation to help stimulate discussion and get people involved at committee meetings, a popular move that led to 200 to 300 people in attendance at every meeting.[27] This appointment enabled her to make contacts with many people she could call on later. In 1988, she chaired the membership committee, and under her leadership, the group added 400 new members to a base of 1,500.[28] Her thirty-three county chairmen became known as her "merry band," providing an esprit de corps she loved. She served on the NMCGA's board of directors from 1984 to 1989 and again from 1992 to 1995. Like her northern New Mexico neighbors, Sammis and Bartley, Thal is active with the New Mexico Association of Conservation Districts and the New Mexico Resources Conservation and Development Council. She especially enjoys these forms of community service, saying, "These are grassroots and local service organizations, which I like. . . . We work with county commissioners, city and state government people for community needs, such as windbreaks, baseball fields, libraries."[29]

Since 1986, one of her most well known and appreciated activist causes has been the development of the Farm and Ranch Heritage Museum, located in southern New Mexico in Las Cruces. In that year, she was selected as one of about 120 ranchers to discuss the feasibility of creating a museum to collect, document, and display the slowly ebbing away history of agriculture in New Mexico. Despite the ranchers' interest, they were unable to find enough financial support for their project, so in 1989, Thal resigned from this committee. Then in 1990, Governor Bruce King stepped in and created the twelve-member Pioneer Board to keep the project alive. He appointed Thal to this committee, and she was quickly

Felicia Thal at the gate to the Thal Ranch, Buena Vista, New Mexico. Courtesy of
Felicia Thal.

elected president. To spur the board into action for their fundraising efforts, Felicia pulled out her checkbook and wrote a personal check for
$1,000 toward their target figure of $70,000, saying, "Here's my thousand
dollars (we needed seventy). I said, come on, seventy more of us and
we've got it done. Four or five at the table put their checks [in]. By the
way, it turned the mood. I said, 'Let's go; let's do it!' And we did it!"[30]

An effective politician when she needed to be, Thal, with the board,
took their proposal to the legislature and successfully lobbied for funds;
they were granted $400,000 initially for architectural design and $7 million later for construction. Groundbreaking took place in August 1995;
the museum opened to great fanfare in 1997 and has proved to be a popular visitor destination. Adjacent to New Mexico State University and its
Department of Agriculture, among other educational assets, the museum
is well situated to promote its mission of education.

Thal is rightfully proud of her efforts in this endeavor, but her family is not surprised at her activist success. Speaking of her Cattleman of
the Year award, her husband, Alan, said, "She is a remarkable woman,
capable of doing anything. She has amazing energy, which she has passed
on to our three children." Her son John adds, "Because of my mother's

enthusiasm for the industry and my father's schedule, which prevented his more active participation, she has been the one involved in much of the public aspect of the cattle industry. She's great at it, and we're very proud of her."[31]

Just as their work on the land brings satisfaction and a sense of well-being, these ranchers and farmers find meaning in service to their local communities also. Most often involved with agricultural issues, in addition to family events such as ball games, dance lessons, school plays, and numerous child-centered activities, the women I talked to loved taking part in community events as well. Serving on the school board, chairing a state committee, testifying before the legislature or Congress, even providing the leadership in establishing a major state museum, Dobbs, Tiegs, Sammis, Bartley, Monzingo, and Thal represent the passion and commitment of ranch and farm women to activist causes that shape their agricultural lifestyle. To echo Mabel Dobbs, "It just gets in your blood."

Epilogue

Ranch families are needed to care for the land in a way that only those who are invested can care.

—Linda Hussa, *The Family Ranch*

The noonday sun glistened on the bright green leaves of the foot-high corn; soybean plants were up four inches, both crops bordering the flat, straight rural road. From the air-conditioned comfort of my rental car, I saw the water tower on the horizon, marking my hometown in east central Illinois. It was Memorial Day weekend, 2010, and I was headed for my fiftieth high school class reunion, back home to my roots. When I started writing this book in the early 2000s, I did not imagine I would feel this homeward pull. After all, I had not lived there since 1961, although I have returned for class reunions every five years since 1980. But in interviewing agricultural women over the past fifteen-plus years, I slowly came to realize that their lives were not that different from the life I had grown up with, and I wanted to acknowledge and celebrate this connection. On top of this, I knew I was really home when, upon entering town, I had to stop and wait on a freight train for ten minutes. Some things don't change much in the countryside, and this small piece of dailyness marked a measure of reassurance.

Some of my classmates were sons and daughters of farmers and patterned their lives similarly. Some of my girlfriends went to college, some did not; some became farmwives and farmers; some followed both paths. Two of them, Maryanne Duncan Johns and Maryann Mooney Mayhall, are in the latter category. Both women grew up in farm families, earned a degree in education, and taught briefly, then "retired" to farm life. Interestingly, neither woman expected to marry a farmer. And although each of them willingly did so, their farm lives took different paths. They graciously agreed to phone interviews after my return to Boise.

Johns grew up on a multigenerational farm where her father grew corn and beans and raised a few cattle and sheep. Her mother had chickens and a garden but also a career as a teacher in the Villa Grove school system. When Maryanne met her husband-to-be, Lyle, he was farming with his brother on leased land; the brothers continue to farm together and have purchased ground (as they say in the Midwest) of their own over the years. After teaching second grade for two years, Maryanne left the profession and gave birth to two sons. She described her life as a "typical" farmwife who served as a "go-fer," took food to the men in the fields, ran the chuckwagon for the combine crew, and drove grain to the local elevator. As expected of most farm women then, she was also responsible for care of the children and home. In many ways, her story reflects the life her western counterparts described to me. Maryanne echoes their sentiments as well. "As a country girl living on a farm, I love it. I couldn't imagine living in town."[1]

Maryann Mooney Mayhall also grew up on a family farm in the same east central region of Illinois.[2] Neither she nor the man she married, Pete Mayhall, thought about being farmers. But after working as an accountant at a local business, Pete decided he preferred to work outdoors, so he joined his dad on their family crop farm. Like her counterpart, Johns, Maryann Mayhall earned a degree in education, but other than a short stint as a teacher's aid when their son, Randy, was in high school, she did not work as a teacher. Instead, she became a farmer, working in partnership with her husband and father-in-law. Very familiar with agricultural equipment, she told me she was happiest when she was plowing farmland in her enclosed and air-conditioned tractor cab, listening to music. The Mayhalls run a technologically progressive farm that today includes machinery that runs on "auto steer," a GPS system based on satellite service.[3] Now, she told me, she has only to "make the turn at the corner." And an iPod has replaced the radio.

As a female farmer, Mayhall carries the double burden of inside as well as outside work, responsible for childcare, cooking, housekeeping, laundry, and the rest. Her fieldwork has diminished as the industry has changed. She "lost" her trucking job when the grain elevator closed and farmers were forced to purchase or hire semitrucks to take their grain to agribusiness giant Cargill's facility nearby. However, she says she has "created a monster" around the noon meal, still carrying it to the men in the fields when most of her farmwife friends tell her they gave up that chore long ago. But like Johns, she wouldn't want to live in town, where "it's too close; I would feel like people were watching me all the time." Maryann loves the freedom she has in the countryside, no eight-to-five jobs, different tasks every day, and planting trees, shrubs, and flowers on the 2 acres surrounding their farmhouse. When I asked her what she likes about her lifestyle, she said, "Smelling the fresh plowed ground or smelling corn when it's pollinating; it's [farming] just in me."

Mayhall and Johns are two of 137,246 women listed as farm operators in the 65-to-74-year-old age group in the most recent agricultural census.[4] This 2007 census figure is nearly 30 percent higher than the 2002 census figure of 94,545. This newest data, released in February of 2009, shows some surprising changes in U.S. agriculture. First, the number of farms has grown 4 percent, and the operators of those farms have become more diverse in the past five years.[5] Women are a part of this diversity, along with increasing numbers of Spanish-speaking, Native American, Asian American, and African American operators. Second, the age of farm operators is increasing at both ends of the spectrum. Of seven age groups, only the 35–44 age category declined, while the other six increased. That means that even my youngest respondent, Terra Graf of Cortez, Colorado, 27 in 2007, is one of an increasing number of younger women operators. Most of my other interviewees fall into the two oldest groups, 65–74 and 75 and over; at least eight of the women I interviewed are 75 or older.

Despite fears of the demise of the family farm, nearly 300,000 new farms have begun operation since the last census. Compared to farms nationwide, these new farms tend to have more diversified production, fewer acres, lower sales, and younger operators who also work off-farm. The figures also show a continuation in the trend toward more small and more very large farms and fewer midsized operations.[6] Compared to all farms nationwide, those with female principal operators tend to be small in terms of both size and sales, although the women are more likely than men to own all of the farmland they operate. They also are more diverse; they are much more likely than men to operate farms classified as "other livestock farms," a category that includes horse farms, or "all other crops," which includes hay farms. Men are more likely to run grain and oilseed farms and beef cattle operations. Again, Graf's work with horses is reflected in this census observation.[7]

One other interesting finding in the 2007 census is that the percentage of women as principal operators by state is highest in the West and New England regions. Arizona is highest in the nation at 38.5 percent; Alaska has 24.5 percent. The Midwest ranks the lowest with 10 percent of all female operators, in just four states: South Dakota (7.7 percent), Nebraska (8.4 percent), Minnesota (9.1 percent), and Iowa (9.1 percent).[8]

Late in September 2010, I attempted to contact many of my interviewees; I reached thirteen women who brought me up to date on their lives. I was saddened to learn of the deaths of three of my earliest contacts: Elizabeth Lloyd, Irene Getz, and Jean Nichols, a Lubbock, Texas, farmer who died in 2005 at age 63. Several of the women "sold out," to either developers or agribusinesses, and moved to town. Some have been widowed, and some continue to live and work on family farms. Here are their updates.

Among my oldest interviewees, 75 or older, that I was able to contact by phone, three (Bartley, Hill, and Monzingo) continue to live on the farm or ranch, and three (Ascuena, Powell, and Helen Tiegs) were living in or have moved to town. They all told me they have slowed down as they've aged but are managing to "get around" to one degree or another. Four of these women were widows when I first interviewed them (Ascuena, Bartley, Powell, and Monzingo); one (Helen Tiegs) has been widowed since we last spoke. Editha Bartley and Peggy Monzingo continue to live on their family properties and play a major role in management decisions; each has a son and daughter-in-law who live on the ranch and provide the labor. Helen Tiegs was widowed in the fall of 2009, but she and her husband had left their crop farm nine years earlier. All of them have family members living on their property or nearby who provide help on many levels.

When I revisited the women by telephone recently, several of the older women spoke excitedly about new activities they are engaged in that link them to their agricultural pasts. They write for local newspapers, are published authors and public speakers, and enjoy taking part in historical reenactments; one woman wrote personal essays and shared them on National Public Radio for twenty years. These ranch and farm women have found new ways of telling their stories in different forms and beyond simple narratives. They work from their lived experiences but deliver it in new or different forms. In continuing to live and tell their stories, they have found new forms of expression or new ways of remembering.[9]

Former "hippie" wife, later ranch woman, Carol Gildesgard serves as a good example. Carol enjoys taking part in historical reenactments in one of the West's most visited and colorful towns, Virginia City, Nevada. Indeed, the town itself is a "reenactment" of this nineteenth-century mining boomtown. The "wrangling women" I discuss in chapter 4 are not exactly performing reenactments but are retelling their lived experiences in a different way. These women work from a familiar body of knowledge, working with and caring for horses, but deliver it in a new form, as part of guided wilderness expeditions.

Two of the ranch women, Felicia Thal and Gretchen Sammis, both of New Mexico, have been active in the establishment and development of the Farm and Ranch Heritage Museum in that state. Museums make it their mission to educate visitors about the past in ways that draw on memory and remembering. Thal's commitment to establishing the New Mexico Farm and Ranch Heritage Museum, and Sammis's contributions as owner of a historical ranch, remind us that using and reusing the past is not always about stories but also about actions. Wilma Powell's induction into the National Cowgirl Museum and Hall of Fame recognizes western lifestyles in an institutional way, one that honors the spirits of those who have participated as ranch and farm women as well as philanthropists, entertainers, artists, competitive performers, writers, and pioneers.

Several of my interviewees identify as writers, sharing their personal experiences through the written word. In writing their stories, they are drawing on their history but delivering it in a new form, in books, in articles, and in public speaking. Since their retirement from farming, Editha Bartley and Lila Hill both write historical material for local news sources. Judy Blunt writes of painful personal experiences that eventually led to her departure from the family ranch; she now teaches at a western university and enjoys a flourishing publishing career. Diane Josephy Peavey, a latecomer to ranching, found an outlet for her stories in a weekly segment on National Public Radio. Peavey is also a published author and sought-after public speaker. As writers and speakers, the women remember and relate their stories in a variety of ways.

Among the older women who have retired from agriculture, two

Carol Gildesgard dressed in her nineteenth-century best as a historical reenactor in Virginia City, Nevada. Courtesy of Carol Gildesgard.

continue to live on the home ranch and two have moved to town to be near other family members. Peggy Monzingo of Benson, Arizona, closed her bed-and-breakfast business about five years ago.[10] Now 88, she told me, "I've had a very stable old age." She misses the stimulation of having guests from faraway places in her home but cannot maintain the same level of cleaning and cooking her B&B required. Since she no longer drives, she is not the activist she once was; she has "pulled in my horns," in her words. She still swims in her backyard pool, and she enjoys being a grandmother but is glad her son and his wife live on the ranch and care for the cattle herd.

When I reconnected with Peggy, she talked about the last few years of drought in the Southwest and how they were forced to reduce the number of cattle on the ranch as a result. But this year has brought abundant spring rains, causing them to think optimistically of restocking some of the cattle. Her son has added windmill work as a supplemental business, more necessary than ever, and hires out to drill wells for other ranchers.

Wilma Powell and her colorful collection of cowgirl boots, much loved and worn daily; Plains, Texas, 1999. Courtesy of Wilma Powell.

The recent moisture has prompted the desert to bloom, and Peggy tells me, "It's a treat to sit here and look out my window at three yucca plants, their white blooms against the western sky. I'm blessed that I can be where I want to be."

When I phoned Peggy's friend in northern New Mexico, Editha Bartley, she told me that at 75, she is still "getting into trouble."[11] She continues to live on the Gascón Ranch with her son and his wife and "tells him what to do." In other words, Editha is still involved with daily ranch decisions, including selling off most of their cattle last year. Now they own just twelve heifers and one bull. They continue to grow and sell Christmas trees and firewood and have added elk hunting to their income source.

Editha was excited to tell me that four years ago she became a columnist for the area newspaper, the *Las Vegas Optic*. In her weekly column, "Palabras Pintorescas" (Word Pictures), she describes her life experiences laced with the history of the region. In addition, she also writes book and restaurant reviews. And finally, as Peggy Monzingo did, she spoke of the "good water El Niño has brought" this spring, with an above-average snowpack of 120 inches in the Sangre de Cristo Mountains. The Gascón Ranch is once again awash in the colors of spring.

Wilma Powell of Plains, Texas, will be 95 years old this coming December and described herself last week as "old and slow."[12] But she, of the colorful custom-made boot collection, is still ordering and wearing boots. She told me that she prefers boots to shoes because she "doesn't fall in boots." I've spoken with Wilma several times since our original interview in 2001 and know that drought and fires in the west Texas plains have wreaked havoc on ranching in the past several years. In 2006, her son Ty and his wife, Linda, who manage the family ranch, sold most of their cattle, and Linda took an off-farm job teaching middle school across the state border in Hobbs, New Mexico. In addition to nature's damage, the Powells were anticipating the possible high cost of identifying each of their cows with an identification number in the wake of the "Mad-Cow Disease" (or BSE) scare that occurred in the 1990s.

In November 2008, Wilma was inducted into the National Cowgirl Museum and Hall of Fame in Fort Worth, a richly deserved honor. The Hall of Fame is the only museum in the world dedicated to honoring and documenting the lives of women who have distinguished themselves while exemplifying the pioneer spirit of the American West. Her award reads:

Carrying on her family's ranching tradition, Wilma is active in community development and preservation of western heritage in the Texas panhandle and northern New Mexico. Wilma supports educating future ranchers in FFA and 4H clubs and is a living example of a lifestyle that has largely disappeared from today's American landscape.[13]

Powell is in good company in the National Cowgirl Museum and Hall of Fame, which includes honorees Annie Oakley, Dale Evans, Patsy Cline, Georgia O'Keeffe, and Sandra Day O'Connor. Powell joins two other women who are subjects in this book, Gretchen Sammis and Ruby Gobble, both of Cimarron, New Mexico. The museum began in the basement of the local library in Hereford, Texas, in the 1970s, moved to Fort Worth in 1994, then into its spacious new building in the Cultural District in 2002. The nearly 200 inductees are "the stuff of legends" —artists and writers, champions and competitive performers, entertainers, ranchers, trailblazers and pioneers. Powell, steward of land and livestock, said she is thrilled and honored to be counted among her peers in the Cowgirl

Hall of Fame. Then she commented on the good ranch conditions at that time, August of 2009. "We got rain, the grass is green, the cattle are fat." Truly a steward of the land.

Sister inductees Gretchen Sammis and Ruby Gobble of the historic Chase family ranch in northern New Mexico are still "carryin' on" with daily ranching activities, Gretchen told me when I called recently. Tight-lipped about her plans for the family property after she passes on, she told me that "people will just have to wait and see when I die." In the meantime, she said, "things are still the same" and added, "Come by and visit again when you're in the area." I look forward to that visit in the near future.[14]

Two farm women west of Boise, Idaho, have been displaced in the dairy business but in different ways. When I called Lila Hill of Meridian, I found that she and her husband still live on the family homestead but have sold their dairy herd, keeping just enough cows to qualify as a farm for county recordkeeping.[15] Their son runs the farm, but they no longer milk for the market. They continue to raise corn, silage, and hay. Lila commented on the reduction in agricultural land in Ada County in the past two decades and the growth of subdivisions, very much a vexing situation for Treasure Valley farmers. At one time, she had feared the new urban growth would bump up against their property line.

Because she is "closer to 80 than 75," she has cut down on the size of her garden and flower beds. And no more piano lessons—she says, "My patience ran out!" She does find great pleasure in serving as the Meridian city historian, a volunteer position that allows her to also write and publish local histories. Lila Hill still finds meaning in the pleasure of a life lived close to the land.

When I first interviewed Helen Tiegs of Nampa, Idaho, a little west and south of Meridian, she saw herself as the "hub of the wheel" that kept the family crop farm running smoothly. But in the mid- to late 1990s, large dairy farms began to move into southern Idaho, buying up small to midsized farms and making Idaho the sixth-largest milk-producing region in the country in 1998.[16] Mostly from California and Washington state, these dairy families were attracted to Idaho because the dairy "infrastructure was already here with the milk processors, dairy equipment suppliers and so on," said the owner of a 1,600-head operation now established in Kuna, south of Boise.[17] Other Idahoans are less convinced by these factors, saying dairies are moving into the state because of weak environmental laws.[18] While there is truth in both statements, dairying has continued to grow in Idaho, particularly the cheese market, where most of Idaho's milk goes. In 2009, the state ranked third in the nation in total cheese production, behind Wisconsin and California.[19]

In 2000, the Tiegses sold their land to a California dairy; soon the new owners put 8,000 cows on 500 acres. Helen told me that "it wasn't a hard decision. Don was ill and on oxygen then and farming's gotten harder. You have to be a big-time farmer now to make a go of it." Their son also sold his farmland, adjacent to his folks' property. The couple moved a few miles closer to town to be near their daughter, Cynthia Tiegs Betz, a teacher in the Nampa school system. This once "hub of the wheel" told me she misses "the wheels of agriculture."

Helen, 81 this year, continues to be an active member in the Idaho Agri-Women organization, although the group now meets sporadically as membership has declined. They continue to fund agricultural scholarships with proceeds from the annual John Deere dinners; Helen enjoys contributing pies. She also is a member of the Bennett Community Club, a group of farmwives in the region who have met monthly over the past seventy-five years. I asked about gardening and flowers, but she has given up that pastime. When her husband died last September, they had been married sixty-two years. She held his service on their anniversary. "It seemed fitting," she said, "a beginning and an end."

Martha Ascuena, of Mountain Home, Idaho, stayed on her beloved ranch for ten years after her husband George died in 1997. In 2007, she moved over 100 miles west to the small town of Weiser to be near her son, who farms nearby. She still drives and loves to visit him on his crop farm. One of her six grandsons lives next door with his family, so she feels cared for and content. The ranch property is still in the family; her stepson and his wife live in the ranch house and lease the land. Instead of cattle, they raise potatoes. Martha hasn't lost her cheerful demeanor, although like some of the other older interviewees, she's "just slower."

Felicia Thal might agree with Martha Ascuena that she, too, has slowed down a bit. When we finally connected by phone, Felicia reported in that wonderfully rich South African accent that things are "pretty much the same" since we last spoke in 2004.[20] She continues to manage the ranch, although they sold their Hereford cattle and lease the land now. Their son Doug, currently an attorney living in Albuquerque, plans to return to the ranch in the near future. Felicia is not as active as she once was, she tells me, having taken herself off most of the community and state boards she once served on. She remains a member of the New Mexico Cattle Growers Association; however, she no longer serves on the board of her once-pet project, the New Mexico Farm and Ranch Heritage Museum in Las Cruces, in southern New Mexico. Felicia is pleased with the development of the museum, now in its sixteenth year, and is happy that younger people are willing to serve as board members. Indeed, she says, "they want 'young blood' and fortunately, there are people willing to do it."

Changes have come for another one of the activist ranch women I interviewed, Mabel Dobbs of Weiser, Idaho.[21] As a hummingbird hovered over the feeder outside the farm kitchen window, Mabel caught me up on their lives in the past six years. In 2004, when the Dobbses' financial condition had improved, Mabel closed down the Family Mortgage Company in Caldwell and returned to the ranch. Also during that year, Mabel and her sister, Jewell Creigh, who had generously helped Grant and Mabel financially during their struggle with lawsuits over property and cattle in the 1990s, decided to start a new business, raising bucking bulls for rodeo use. Grant, who is 76 now and "a wreck" from his years as a bull rider, was enthusiastic, as were other members of their extended family including Creigh's son, Tim Roberts, a bull rider currently on the rodeo circuit.

In 2009, the economic downturn forced the Dobbses to sell their Longhorn herd, though they "still have a few of the old girls as field ornaments." They maintain the bucking bull business, and Mabel and Grant attend many rodeos. She also took a part-time job at the Wells Fargo Bank in nearby Weiser; the lack of commute pleases her as much as the paycheck. Now she is "enjoying very much watching the granddaughters clog dance, play baseball and basketball."

Dobbs is still very engaged in rural activist issues, especially with the Idaho Rural Council, where she chairs the Livestock Committee. She told me that she "hope[s] to see a viable group before I get uninvolved, [working] on multi-faceted rural issues. It's critical; if we don't step up to the plate and take up the challenge . . . " Her voice trails off. I asked her how she sees the future for U.S. agriculture. She replied:

> I think that what you're going to see, and I'm seeing it now, is more
> of a coming back of more local [form of agriculture]. I think you're

Mabel Dobbs and author at the Dobbs Ranch, Weiser, Idaho, 2010. Courtesy of Mabel Dobbs.

going to see more people growing a garden. Not only because of the need to do that but from just the food safety stuff alone. People are becoming a little more aware of where that food is coming from, how that food is grown, what's in that food that we're eating. Back to more of a local, regional food base . . . that over the last fifteen to twenty years, we've gotten so far away from. . . . The work groups over the past five or six years have been talking very intently about local foods, food safety, food security, which, in turn, then come back to the fact that you may very well see these smaller, small-sized farm operations that will be able to make a little more viable living than they have before.

Terra Graf, the youngest farm woman at the time of our interview in 2002, is 30 now and has seen some changes in her life since then. First, she and her husband sold their herd, and she now works with her parents, her brother, and a few neighbors on their farms near Cortez, Colorado. She told me she still works with horses but is no longer one of southern Colorado's two brand inspectors since there is no longer enough work for two people. Her husband, Terrill, continues to work as a welder, and Terra herself has taken a job in town. She works nights as a lab technician and "doesn't really care for it." But, as for many farm operators, it provides additional income until the time when, or if, the couple can return to farming full-time.

She sounded somewhat wistful as she told me she had helped move cows that day. When I inquired about her neighbor and friend Marion Kelley, Terra reported that Marion's husband, John, died last year, so she sold their cows and leased out the ranch. She still lives in the farm house, but according to Terra, she leased her pasture to the men who bought her cattle "so she sees them often."

When I caught up with Carol Gildesgard, she had just taken part in a reenactment skit in Virginia City, Nevada, where she is a member of the Horse Thief Canyon Desperadoes.[22] Although her day job is real estate, she enjoys getting into western garb and Civil War–era ballgowns and reliving the past. Despite the fact that she did not grow up in agriculture, her adult life in Montana as a wife and mother made a deep impact. She believes that the difficult environment there shaped her life and her role in that setting, and she misses it. "It is a pull, but you don't often realize it until later in life," she told me.

Carol Inouye voiced a similar refrain.[23] Carol and husband Chris raised two children and row crops in Parma, Idaho, near the Oregon border. Neither of the children cared to take over the farm, so in 2002, they had a farm sale and retired to Caldwell, 40 miles southwest of Boise. They kept 20 acres and built a house, and now Chris plants—landscapes, Carol called it on a smaller scale. Carol laughed as she told me, "You can't, you don't get agriculture out of your veins." Carol had just returned from Los Angeles, where she had taken part in a new intellectual movement that brings people together for thoughtful discussions called "Intentional Conversations." She hopes to initiate a similar movement in the Treasure Valley. "Life is exciting after agriculture," she said. Still, she pointed out that they had built their house on top of a hill and "still watch the weather."

Like nature writer Linda Hasselstrom, Diane Josephy Peavey now spends her days writing and ranching. Her twenty-year radio program ended two years ago; you can read many of those "tiny stories" in her recent publication, *Bitterbrush Country*. In December 2009, Peavey was honored as one of ten Women of Today by the Girl Scouts of the Silver Sage Council in the Treasure Valley. In her acceptance speech, Diane talked about the importance of story: "Learning stories and sharing them with others, in my case through my writings, has become a driving force in my life."[24] Then she shared a humorous bit of her introduction to life on the Flat Top Sheep Ranch.

On my first month at the ranch I was asked to help with the branding. I had four choices of jobs, I was told: I could shoot ear tags into the calves' ears (I never liked getting my own ears pierced); give them injections (who likes getting or giving shots?); brand them (the smell of burning hair already had me reeling); or—I held out for the fourth option—I could castrate them. I grabbed a fence post for support, thinking I might pass out. "Could I hear those four options again?" I whispered.[25]

Telling stories, ways of remembering, has nearly as many facets as the speakers themselves. The women I interviewed told me their stories and how they remember them in a variety of ways. They recited their daily chores in lively narrative fashion; they spoke of becoming business-women on dude ranches and bed-and-breakfast inns as a way to share the western lifestyle; they told of the hard work and the pleasure they find in wrangling horses, cooking meals, and telling stories on wilderness trips; they adopt historical personas as reenactment participants; and they share their experiences as published authors and public speakers. They remind us who we are, where we have been, how we got there, and what happened on the way. They bring us joy as well as sadness, link us as families, as friends, and inspire new relationships. I hope the stories you have read here will inspire you for all these reasons and more. Remember, if you don't tell your stories, who will?

Ranch/Farm Women Questionnaire

BACKGROUND INFORMATION

Date of birth

Family background, length of time in state

Family size; siblings, ages

Number of children, sex, birthdates

Education

FARM/RANCH HISTORY

Do you refer to your operation as a ranch or a farm?

How do you refer to yourself?

Did you grow up on a farm?

How many years have you lived or worked on a ranch/farm?

Do you consider yourself to be the main operator or one of the main operators for the ranch/farm? (By operator, I mean the person who makes day-to-day decisions about running the operation.)

Do you rent or lease land from others? If so, how many acres?

Is your name on the deed, title, lease or rental contract for any of this land?

Do you raise crops or livestock or a combination of both?

What are they?

Does farming/ranching sustain your way of life?

If not, do you or someone else work off the farm/ranch for wages?

If so, how much would you say these wages contribute to the ranch/farm income?

FARM/RANCH WORK

Regarding outside work:

How involved are you in planting, plowing, disking, or cultivation of your crops?

Applying fertilizers, herbicides, or insecticides?

Doing other fieldwork without machinery?

Harvesting crops or other products, including running machinery or driving farm equipment?

Taking care of farm animals, including herding or milking dairy cattle?

Running farm errands, such as picking up repair parts or supplies?

Making major purchases of farm or ranch supplies and equipment?

Marketing your products—that is, dealing with wholesale buyers or selling directly to consumers?

Regarding inside work:

How involved are you in household work such as cooking, cleaning, laundry, sewing/mending, or childcare?

Taking care of a vegetable garden or animals for family consumption?

Supervising the farmwork of other farm members?

Supervising the work of hired farm labor?

Working on a family or in-home business other than farm/ranch work?

Bookkeeping, maintaining records, paying bills, or preparing tax forms for the operation?

DECISION MAKING

Who usually makes the decision to:

Buy or sell land?

Buy major household appliances?

Buy major farm equipment?

Produce something new such as a new crop or a new breed or type of livestock?

Sell your products?

Take a job off the farm/ranch?

Make household repairs or improvements?

Has there been anyone besides you or your husband/partner who has regularly helped make these kinds of decisions for your operation? Who is that person(s)?

In general, thinking about the part you play in making decisions for the operation of this farm/ranch, do you feel that you have too much responsibility, or would you like to have a greater part in decision making?

If something should happen to your husband/partner, could you continue to run the operation on your own?

How will the land be divided among heirs? Is this a controversial topic among family members?

FAMILY, FRIENDS, AND COMMUNITY

Do you have other family members living nearby?

How often do you get together?

Could you go to family members if you need help? Money?

Do family members come to you for help?

Were your babies born in the hospital? With a midwife? Did you have help from mother, sister, friends in childbirth?

Are there opportunities for women to get together as friends?

What activities do you do together?

What kinds of things do you talk about when you get together with friends? Consider these topics: work, children, husbands, gossip, politics, religion, advice. Anything else?

Where did you go to school? Church? Shopping? Visiting?

Do you belong to any clubs? 4-II? Agricultural Extension Service? Homemaker clubs? Farm Bureau Women, Cowbelles, or any other farm/ranch associations?

Have you ever displayed any products at a county or state fair?

What newspapers and magazines does your family read?

What television programs do you watch?

Do you have a computer in your farm/ranch home? Who uses it? In what ways?

POST—WORLD WAR II

Here I am interested in conditions for farm/ranch women in the late 1940s, 1950s, and 1960s.

How would you say your life changed most drastically in these years?

Did you have indoor plumbing? Electricity? Telephone service?

Did you buy new items for the farm/ranch such as large equipment?

Did you buy new items for the house? Television? Home food freezer? Washer or dryer? Furniture?

How were the decisions to buy new items made? By you? Husband/partner? Together?

Were you satisfied/pleased with this method?

Did you wish your farm/ranch had as many amenities as those who lived in town?

What did you miss most, if anything, by living in a rural area?

How satisfied are you with ranching/farming as a way of life?

As a way to make a living?

Are you aware of the women's movement that appeared in the last third of the twentieth century? What do you know about this topic? How has it affected you or what you do?

If you have experienced a divorce, are you willing to discuss it here? What kinds of problems did you experience afterward? Has divorce changed your lifestyle on the farm/ranch?

Regarding widowhood: how did your life and work change at the death of your spouse/partner?

Are there other stories or information you would like to add?

Thank you very much for taking part in this interview.

Interviewees

Ascuena, Martha, Mountain Home, Idaho
Bartley, Editha, Rociada, New Mexico
Betz, Cynthia Tiegs, Meridian, Idaho
Betz, Eldon, Meridian, Idaho
Dobbs, Mabel, Weiser, Idaho
Evans, Clint, Garden Valley, Idaho
Evans, Eilene, Garden Valley, Idaho
Gildesgard, Carol, Reno, Nevada
Gobble, Ruby, Cimarron, New Mexico
Graf, Terra, Lewis, Colorado
Hill, Lila, Meridian, Idaho
Holtschlag, Kali, Dragoon, Arizona
Inouye, Carol, Parma, Idaho
Jeffries, Barbara, Durango, Colorado
Johns, Maryanne Duncan, Tuscola, Illinois
Kelley, Marion, Durango, Colorado
Lloyd, Elizabeth, Boise, Idaho
Mayhall, Maryann Mooney, Camargo, Illinois
Monzingo, Peggy, Benson, Arizona
Murgoitio, Linda, Meridian, Idaho
Nichols, Jean, Idalou, Texas
Ortega, Sylvia, Guadalupita, New Mexico
Peavey, Diane Josephy, Carey, Idaho
Powell, Wilma, Plains, Texas
Romero, Rosalie, Chacón, New Mexico
Sammis, Gretchen, Cimarron, New Mexico
Tadano, Michiko, Glendale, Arizona
Thal, Felicia, Buena Vista, New Mexico
Tiegs, Helen, Meridian, Idaho
Trambley, Alice, Mora, New Mexico
Trambley, Frank, Mora, New Mexico

Notes

PREFACE

1. The Centennial Farms Program honors generations of farmers who have worked to maintain family farms in Illinois. To qualify for Centennial Farm status, an agricultural property must have been owned by the same family of lineal or collateral descendants for at least 100 years. Families who qualify receive an official Centennial Farm sign suitable for outdoor display. My aunt and uncle lived on this property from 1966 until 1990; their sign was prominently displayed in the farm home living room.

2. Sandra Schackel, "Ranch and Farm Women in the Contemporary American West," in *The Rural West since World War II*, ed. R. Douglas Hurt, 99–118 (Lawrence: University Press of Kansas, 1998).

CHAPTER 1. I'D RATHER BE ON THE FARM

1. Helen Tiegs, Nampa, Idaho, interview by author, June 29, 1995.

2. Martha Ascuena, Mountain Home, Idaho, interview by author, June 26, 1995.

3. Carol Inouye, Parma, Idaho, interview by author, January 29, 1996.

4. Linda M. Hasselstrom, *Between Grass and Sky: Where I Live and Work* (Las Vegas: University of Nevada Press, 2002). See her introduction.

5. Rena Sanderson, "Linda Hasselstrom: The Woman Rancher as Nature Writer," in *Such News of the Land: U.S. Women Nature Writers*, ed. Thomas S. Edwards and Elizabeth A. De Wolfe (Hanover, N.H.: University Press of New England, 2001), 170–177.

6. Linda Hasselstrom, *Windbreak: A Woman Rancher on the Northern Plains* (Berkeley, Calif.: Barn Owl Books, 1987), xi.

7. Ibid., 88–89.

8. Jefferson wrote that the "cultivators of the earth are the most valuable citizens . . . the most independent, the most virtuous, and they are tied to their country and wedded to its liberty and interest by the most lasting bonds." He believed that as long as people could own their own farms, they would, by virtue of hard work, provide for the basic necessities of life. The agrarian way of life, in turn,

would produce virtuous citizens, essential to the survival of the Republic. This agrarian view would, however, gradually diminish as western lands were slowly taken up and the nation's population continued to grow, leading in the twentieth century to the dominance of an urban population. Jefferson's quotes are from Pauline Maier, et al., *Inventing America: A History of the United States,* vol. 1 (New York: W. W. Norton, 2003), 286, 374.

9. See USDA, *The Census of Agriculture,* http://www.agcensus.usda.gov, for data in this chapter. See the epilogue for the most recent census figures, the Agriculture Census of 2007.

10. Rachel Rosenfeld, *Farm Women: Work, Farm, and Family in the United States* (Chapel Hill: University of North Carolina Press, 1985), 12–13.

11. Ibid.

12. Nancy Woloch, *Women and the American Experience,* 3rd ed. (New York: Alfred A. Knopf, 2000), 471–485.

13. William H. Chafe, *The Paradox of Change: American Women in the 20th Century* (New York: Oxford University Press, 1991), 167–168.

14. Elizabeth Maret describes this term as "the fine art of finding everything needed." See *Women of the Range: Women's Roles in the Texas Beef Cattle Industry.* (College Station: Texas A&M University Press, 1993), 38.

15. Carlos Schwantes, *In Mountain Shadows: A History of Idaho* (Lincoln: University of Nebraska Press, 1991), 166.

16. Population figures from ibid., 228, 224, respectively.

17. These once stable and "homegrown" companies have all faced serious business challenges in the first decade of the twenty-first century. Micron is no longer the world's leading chip maker; the Albertsons supermarket chain was sold and its headquarters moved to Minneapolis; Boise Cascade dropped Boise from its name; Hewlett-Packard made cutbacks when they acquired Compaq; and Washington Group International was acquired by URS, an engineering and construction company based in San Francisco.

18. Her family was not involved in internment. They were part of a few families who had settled in this area (eastern Oregon, western Idaho) in the twenties and were not considered a threat because they lived so far from the coast.

19. Cynthia and Eldon Betz, Nampa, Idaho, interview by author, September 19, 2004.

20. Terra Graf and Marion Kelley, Durango, Colorado, interview by author, October 8, 2002.

21. Marion Kelley, Durango, Colorado, interview by author, October 7, 2002.

22. Carol Gildesgard, Reno, Nevada, interview by author in Elko, Nevada, February 4, 2007.

23. "Felicia Thal: Cattleman of the Year," *New Mexico Stockman*, November 1993, 82–88.

CHAPTER 2. I'D RATHER WORK OUTSIDE THAN DO HOUSEWORK

1. Judy Blunt, *Breaking Clean* (New York: Vintage Books, 2003), 210.

2. Ibid., 211.

3. Ibid., 4.

4. Ibid., 202–203. In the 1970s, government policies encouraged farmers to increase their land holdings and plant "fencerow to fencerow." By the end of the decade, the axiom had become, "Get bigger, get better, or get out." R. Douglas Hurt, *Problems of Plenty: The American Farmer in the Twentieth Century* (Chicago: Ivan R. Dee, 2002), 132–134.

5. Nancy Grey Osterud, "Gender and the Transition to Capitalism in Rural America," *Agricultural History* 67 (Spring 1993): 14–29.

6. Katherine Jellison, *Entitled to Power: Farm Women and Technology, 1913–1963* (Chapel Hill: University of North Carolina Press, 1993), 169–170.

7. Rosalie Romero, Chacon, New Mexico, interview by author, October 3, 1995.

8. Jean Nichols, Idalou, Texas, interview by author, June 20, 2001.

9. William H. Chafe, *The Paradox of Change: American Women in the 20th Century* (New York: Oxford University Press, 1991). See ch. 9, "The Paradox of Change," 154–172.

10. Ibid., 166.

11. Kali Holtschlag, Benson, Arizona, interview by author, May 16, 1996.

12. Peggy Monzingo, Benson, Arizona, interview by author May 16, 1996.

13. Mary Neth, *Preserving the Family Farm: Women, Community, and the Foundations of Agribusiness in the Midwest, 1900–1940* (Baltimore: Johns Hopkins University Press, 1995), 215.

14. Zoe Murphy, "Does Your Wife/Husband Help?" *Wallaces' Farmer*, September 20, 1958, 60.

15. Ibid.

16. Carolyn E. Sachs, *The Invisible Farmer: Women in Agricultural Production* (Totowa, N.J.: Rowman and Allanheld, 1983).

17. Elizabeth Lloyd, Boise, Idaho, interview by author, September 18, 1995.

18. Martha Ascuena, Mountain Home, Idaho, interview by author, June 26, 1995.

19. Linda Murgoitio, Meridian, Idaho, interview by author, September 20, 1995.

20. Sarah Elbert, "Women and Farming: Changing Structures, Changing

Roles," in *Women and Farming: Changing Roles, Changing Structures,* ed. Wava G. Haney and Jane B. Knowles (Boulder, Colo.: Westview Press, 1988), 161–162.

21. Elizabeth Maret, *Women of the Range: Women's Roles in the Texas Beef Cattle Industry* (College Station: Texas A&M University Press, 1993), xiii.

22. Ibid., 7–8.

23. Ibid., 34–35.

24. Wilma Luna Powell, Plains, Texas, interview by author, May 7, 2001.

25. Wilma explained this term to me: "You say that when you moved your cookin' utensils, you've moved your skillet" to a new location or kitchen.

26. Felicia Thal, Buena Vista, New Mexico, interview by author, September 14, 1995.

27. "Felicia Thal: Cattleman of the Year," *New Mexico Stockman,* November 1993, 82–88.

28. Ibid., 83.

29. Sharon Niederman, "Three Ranch Women," *Cowboys and Indians* 5 (Spring 1995): 34.

30. Ibid.

CHAPTER 3. I DIDN'T MILK COWS; I GAVE PIANO LESSONS

1. Lila Hill, Meridian, Idaho, interview by author, September 13, 1995.

2. Elizabeth Lloyd, Boise, Idaho, interview by author, September 18, 1995.

3. Katherine Jellison, *Entitled to Power: Farm Women and Technology, 1913–1963* (Chapel Hill: University of North Carolina Press, 1993).

4. Elaine Tyler May, *Homeward Bound: American Families in the Cold War Era* (New York: Basic Books, 1988), 165.

5. Ibid.

6. Susan M. Hartmann, *The Home Front and Beyond: American Women in the 1940s* (Boston: Twayne Publishers, 1982), 8.

7. In 1936, as part of FDR's New Deal, Congress passed the Rural Electrification Act (REA), creating a federal agency charged with providing electrical service to rural areas. To do so, the federal government made loans available to state and local governments and farmers' cooperatives. By the early 1970s, 98 percent of farms in the United States had electrical service.

8. U.S. Bureau of the Census, *Statistical Abstract of the United States: 1957,* 78th ed. (Washington, D.C.: Government Printing Office, 1957), 641.

9. Jellison, *Entitled to Power,* 150.

10. Ibid.

11. Martha Ascuena, Mountain Home, Idaho, interview by author, June 26, 1995.

12. Jellison, *Entitled to Power*, 166.

13. Rosalie Romero, Chacon, New Mexico, interview by author, October 3, 1995.

14. Linda Murgoitio, Meridian, Idaho, interview by author, September 29, 1995.

15. Terra Graf, Cortez, Colorado, interview by author, October 8, 2002.

16. Helen Tiegs, Nampa, Idaho, interview by author, June 29, 1995.

17. Ascuena interview.

18. Lloyd interview.

19. Diane Josephy Peavey, Carey, Idaho, interview with author, December 4–5, 2002.

20. Pat Murphy, "Flat Top Sheep Ranch: Peavey Country as Far as the Eye Can See," *Idaho Mountain Express*, October 20–26, 1999.

21. See ch. 4 for discussion of IRC.

22. Her weekly essays have since been published in *Bitterbrush Country: Living on the Edge of the Land* (Golden, Colo.: Fulcrum Publishing, 2001).

23. Jellison, *Entitled to Power*, 170–173.

24. Ibid., 171.

25. Ibid.

26. Ibid., 173.

27. William deBuys, *Enchantment and Exploitation: The Life and Hard Times of a New Mexico Mountain Range* (Albuquerque: University of New Mexico Press, 1985), 211.

28. Romero interview.

29. Alice and Frank Trambley, Mora, New Mexico, interview by author, October 3, 1995.

30. Cornelia Butler Flora and Jan L. Flora, "Structure of Agriculture and Women's Culture in the Great Plains," *Great Plains Quarterly* 8 (Fall 1988): 195–205.

31. Ibid., 197.

32. Madeline Buckendorf, "The Poultry Frontier: Family Farm Roles and Turkey Raising in Southwest Idaho, 1910–1940," *Idaho Yesterdays* 37 (Summer 1993): 2–8. See also Joan Jensen, *With These Hands: Women Working on the Land* (Old Westbury, N.Y.: Feminist Press, 1981).

33. Flora and Flora, "Structure of Agriculture and Women's Culture in the Great Plains," 197–198.

34. Sylvia Ortega, Guadalupita, New Mexico, interview by author, October 4, 1995.

35. Barbara Jeffries, Durango, Colorado, interview by author, October 7, 2002.

36. Carol Inouye, Parma, Idaho, interview by author, January 29, 1996.

37. Romero interview.

CHAPTER 4. WE'D BE IN BAD SHAPE IF IT WASN'T FOR HUNTING

1. Lawrence R. Borne, *Dude Ranching: A Complete History* (Albuquerque: University of New Mexico Press, 1983).

2. Theodore Roosevelt, *Ranch Life and the Hunting-Trail* (New York: Century Company, 1899).

3. John A. Murray, *Mythmakers of the West: Shaping America's Imagination* (Flagstaff, Ariz.: Northland Publishing, 2001), 154.

4. John D. Seelye, *Memory's Nation: The Place of Plymouth Rock* (Durham: University of North Carolina Press, 1998). Seelye notes that the first mention of Plymouth Rock in print did not appear until 1775.

5. Joan M. Jensen, *Calling This Place Home: Women on the Wisconsin Frontier, 1850–1925* (St. Paul: Minnesota Historical Society Press, 2006).

6. Earl Pomeroy, *In Search of the Golden West: The Tourist in Western America* (New York: Alfred A. Knopf, 1957).

7. Susan Rhoades Neel, "Tourism and the American West: New Departures," *Pacific Historical Review* 65 (November 1996): 517–523.

8. Hal K. Rothman, "Selling the Meaning of Place: Tourism, Entrepreneurship, and Community Transformation in the Twentieth-Century American West," *Pacific Historical Review* 65 (November 1996).

9. Steven Stoll, *U.S. Environmentalism since 1945: A Brief History with Documents* (Boston: Bedford/St. Martin's, 2007), 6.

10. Quoted in David M. Wrobel and Patrick T. Long, eds., *Seeing and Being Seen: Tourism in the American West* (Lawrence: University Press of Kansas, 2001), 3.

11. Hal K. Rothman, "Introduction: Tourism and the Future," in *The Culture of Tourism, the Tourism of Culture: Selling the Past to the Present in the American Southwest,* ed. Hal K. Rothman (Albuquerque: University of New Mexico Press, 2003), 1–3.

12. Gretchen Sammis, Cimarron, New Mexico, interview by author, October 2, 1995.

13. Transcript from Barbara Van Cleve, *Hard Twist: Western Ranch Women* (Santa Fe: Museum of New Mexico Press, 1995), interview with Ruby Gobble by Barbara Van Cleve.

14. Ibid., 90.

15. Ibid., transcript.

16. Ibid., 89.

17. Editha Bartley, Rociada, New Mexico, interview by author, October 5, 1995. James and Editha's business card reads "Cattle, Guest Ranch, Timber Products."

18. By the early twentieth century, New Mexico had become a mecca for tuberculosis patients seeking a "salubrious" climate in which to recover from their illnesses. According to Joan Jensen, Catholic hospitals took the lead in establishing TB facilities around the state, in Albuquerque, Silver City, Santa Fe, Socorro, Las Vegas, Raton, Las Cruces, and Roswell. Joan M. Jensen, "Silver City Health Tourism in the Early Twentieth Century," *New Mexico Historical Review* 84 (Summer 2009): 321–361. For an overview of this form of "health tourism," see Nancy Owen Lewis, "Chasing the Cure in New Mexico: The Lungers and Their Legacy," *El Palacio* 113, no. 4 (Winter 2008). Despite financial setbacks, Brown was finally able to build the Valmora sanatorium in northern New Mexico, which then provided the opportunity for a guest resort nearby for patients and doctors and their friends. Jensen also discusses TB sanatoriums as part of health tourism in central Wisconsin in *Calling This Place Home.*

19. Borne, *Dude Ranching,* 6–7, 121–122.

20. Kristin M. McAndrews, *Wrangling Women: Humor and Gender in the American West* (Reno: University of Nevada Press, 2006).

21. Ibid., 2, 86, 121.

22. Peggy Monzingo, Benson, Arizona, interview by author, May 17, 1996.

23. David Moore, "Head 'em Out," *New Mexico Magazine,* March 2009, 44–51.

24. Ibid., 47.

25. Ibid., 51.

26. Phone call with Eilene and Clint Evans, December 16, 2009. See their Web site at elk4sale@elk4sale.net.

27. Telephone conversation with Clint Evans, Garden Valley, Idaho, December 16, 2009.

CHAPTER 5. EAT MORE BEEF

1. Mabel Dobbs, Caldwell, Idaho, interview by author July 10, July 21, August 1, 2002.

2. Joan M. Jensen, in *Calling This Place Home: Women on the Wisconsin Frontier, 1850-1925* (St. Paul: Minnesota Historical Society Press, 2006), documents the public and political roles of central Wisconsin women, including Native American women as members of Indian-rights organizations, in establishing rural women's clubs, boys' and girls' clubs, and suffragist organizations. See ch. 8, "Political Landscapes." Over the twentieth century, women gradually expanded their community involvement beyond traditional domestic issues to broader political topics, especially in the postwar era.

3. Women, and men, join associations for many reasons, including gender, in

which they identify as women first, and second as farm workers/owners/opera-tors. And more importantly, they sense revolutionary changes in their way of life, represented in the rapid growth of urbanization and agribusiness.

4. In 1963, Congress passed the Equal Pay Act, the first federal law against sex discrimination and the first to recognize women's status as wage earners since WWII. Nancy Woloch, *Women and the American Experience*, 4th ed. (Boston: McGraw-Hill, 2006). See chs. 19, 20.

5. Mabel Dobbs, Weiser, Idaho, interview by author, July 10, 2002.

6. Ibid.

7. Ibid.

8. *Weiser Signal American*, April 15, 2002.

9. Ibid.

10. The Idaho Rural Council (IRC), was formed in 1986 in response to the farm crisis in southern Idaho. IRC operated at first primarily as a one-on-one counseling and referral organization focused on debt issues during the farm cri-sis. More recently, IRC serves as a grassroots organization to encourage farmers, ranchers, rural community members, churches, and civic groups to get active and become empowered on a variety of issues.

11. The Western Organization of Resource Councils, headquartered in Billings, Montana, formed in the 1970s as a regional network of grassroots community or-ganizations committed to advancing the vision of a democratic, sustainable, and just society through community action. WORC provides training and coordi-nates work around relevant issues for members in Idaho, the Dakotas, Montana, Colorado, and Oregon. Dobbs served on this board for ten years. See their Web site: http://www.worc.org/.

12. The National Cattlemen's Beef Association is the most recent incarnation of a marketing and trade association established in 1898 in Denver, Colorado. During the twentieth century, the association merged twice with other beef-related interest groups, creating the present organization, the NCBA, in 1996. Today it represents more than 230,000 cattle breeders, producers, and feeders, including 28,000 individual members and 64 state affiliate members. Web site: http://www.beefusa.org/.

13. Dobbs is speaking of Dan Glickman, secretary of agriculture during the Clinton administration, 1981–1989.

14. R-CALF USA is a national, nonprofit organization dedicated to ensur-ing the continued profitability and viability of the U.S. cattle industry. R-CALF USA represents thousands of U.S. cattle producers on trade and marketing is-sues. Members are located across forty-seven states and are primarily cow/calf

operators, cattle backgrounders, and/or feedlot owners. Web site: http://www.r-calfusa.com/.

15. A checkoff is a $1.00 fee assessed per head of cattle or sheep or other agricultural product that is used by the industry to promote that product. As Mabel explains, many operators resent this required tax and prefer it to be voluntary.

16. Since 1947, the Livestock Marketing Association has served as the leading advocate for the livestock marketing industry, serving as the voice for local livestock auction markets on state and federal legislative and regulatory issues. Livestock auctions are a vital part of the livestock industry, serving producers and assuring a fair, competitive price through the auction method of selling. Web site: http://www.lmaweb.com/.

17. Lee Pitts, *Livestock Market Digest*, July 15, 2001.

18. Dobbs interview.

19. In 1974, agricultural women in four states—Oregon, Michigan, Wisconsin, and Washington—founded American Agri-Women to provide a single voice in which to respond to problems in the industry. Illinois and Kansas women joined soon after. Today there are fifty state and commodity affiliate organizations as well as individual members numbering in the tens of thousands. Their purpose is to become actively involved in legislative and regulatory matters at the local, state, and national levels. Web site: http://www.americanagriwomen.org/.

20. Helen Tiegs, Nampa, Idaho, interview by author, June 29, 1995.

21. Gretchen Sammis, Cimarron, New Mexico, interview by author, October 2, 1995.

22. In response to the damaging dust storms of the early 1930s, President Franklin D. Roosevelt made conservation a top New Deal priority. In 1935, Congress enacted the Soil Conservation Act, which enabled the federal government to tackle the problem of soil erosion on a national scale. States began to organize into soil conservation districts, and by 1946, when the National Association of Conservation Districts (NACD) was formed, over 1,600 soil conservation districts had already formed in forty-eight states. The NACD helps farmers and ranchers develop conservation plans that provide for sound land use, the proper combination of conservation practices, and improvement of soil productivity. Web site: http://www.nacdnet.org/.

23. Today there are nearly 3,000 conservation districts—one in almost every county. Now expanded to serve all the conservation needs of our nation, districts educate and help local citizens conserve land, water, forests, wildlife, and other natural resources (http://www.nacdnet.org/about/).

24. Editha Bartley, Rociada, New Mexico, interview by author, October 5, 1995.

25. Peggy Monzingo, Benson, Arizona, interview by author, May 17, 1996.

26. The Taylor Grazing Act was passed in 1934 with the mandate of preventing overgrazing on public rangelands. In an effort to establish better environmental management of the Great Plains, FDR created several New Deal agencies, including the popular Civilian Conservation Corps, the Grazing Service (renamed the Bureau of Land Management, or BLM, in 1946), and in 1935, the Soil Conservation Service. The term "enclosure" refers to federal lands fenced off from public use to allow overgrazed acreage to recover.

27. "Felicia Thal: Cattleman of the Year," *New Mexico Stockman,* November 1993, 82–88.

28. Sharon Niederman, "Three Ranch Women," *Cowboys and Indians* 5 (Spring 1995): 29–34.

29. "Felicia Thal: Cattleman of the Year," 84.

30. Felicia Thal, Buena Vista, New Mexico, interview by author, October 4, 1995.

31. "Felicia Thal: Cattleman of the Year," 82, 87.

EPILOGUE

1. Maryanne Duncan Johns, Tuscola, Illinois, telephone interview by author, June 4, 2010.

2. Maryann Mooney Mayhall, Villa Grove, Illinois, telephone interview by author, June 10, 2010.

3. "High-Tech Harvest: Tools Alter How Farmers Do Their Job," *Idaho Statesman,* September 12, 2008, 1, 4, section B.

4. The narrative above is from USDA, "Census of Agriculture Shows Growing Diversity in U.S. Farming," February 4, 2009, http://www.usda.gov/wps/portal/usda/usdahome?contentidonly=true&contentid=2009/02/0036.xml. Other census information is also available at http://www.usda.gov.

5. The 2007 census counted 2,204,792 farms in the United States, a 4 percent increase from 2002. The number of farms nationwide has been on a declining trend since World War II. This latest figure indicates a leveling of the trend, with a net increase of 75,810 farms. Ibid. More recently, an online newsletter, *Harvest Public Media,* reports that women are the fastest growing groups among minority farmers, a 30% increase since 2002. Women currently operate 300,000 farms, 14% of the nation's total. Rather than grow row crops, such as corn or soybeans, women are more likely to raise livestock and grow organic vegetables. Women are also taking the lead in growing sustainable food products for the growing local food movement. Kathleen Masterson, February 22, 2011. http://harvestpublicmedia.org.

6. Large family farms (with sales between $250,000 and $500,000) and very large family farms (sales over $500,000) made up only 9 percent of all farms. Yet they produced more than 63 percent of the value of all agricultural products sold. Ibid.

7. "Women," Agriculture Census of 2007, February 2009.

8. Ibid.

9. I wish to thank Joan Jensen, a pioneer in the field of agricultural women and gracious mentor to many, for her use and explanation of this term, "ways of remembering," and its usefulness in describing the lives of many of my informants today. Telephone conversation with author, August 25, 2010.

10. Peggy Monzingo, Benson, Arizona, telephone interview by author, June 13, 2010.

11. Editha Bartley, Rociada, New Mexico, telephone interview by author, May 23, 2010.

12. Wilma Powell, Plains, Texas, telephone interview by author, June 13, 2010.

13. See the Web site: http://cowgirl.net/home/home/hall-of-fame/.

14. Gretchen Sammis, Cimarron, New Mexico, telephone interview by author, May 28, 2010.

15. Lila Hill, Meridian, Idaho, telephone interview by author, June 7, 2010.

16. "California Pushes out Dairy Farms," *Idaho Statesman,* September 6, 1998, 1, 4, section D.

17. Ibid.

18. Ibid.

19. "Idaho Dairies Struggle to Hang On," *Idaho Statesman,* April 13, 2010, 1, 4, section A.

20. Felicia Thal, Buena Vista, New Mexico, telephone interview by author, June 12, 2010.

21. Mabel Dobbs, Weiser, Idaho, interview by author, May 25, 2010.

22. Carol Gildesgard, Reno, Nevada, June 9, 2010, telephone interview by author.

23. Carol Inouye, Caldwell, Idaho, June 7, 2010, telephone interview by author.

24. Diane Ronayne, "'Women of Today' Honoree Shares Her Story," *Idaho Statesman,* December 6, 2009, C5.

25. Ibid.

Selected Bibliography

Blunt, Judy. *Breaking Clean.* New York: Vintage Books, 2003.

Borne, Lawrence R. *Dude Ranching: A Complete History.* Albuquerque: University of New Mexico Press, 1983.

Buckendorf, Madeline. "The Poultry Frontier: Family Farm Roles and Turkey Raising in Southwest Idaho, 1910–1940." *Idaho Yesterdays* 37 (Summer 1993): 2–8.

"California Pushes Out Dairy Farms." *Idaho Statesman,* September 6, 1998, 1, 4, section D.

Chafe, William. *The Paradox of Change: American Women in the 20th Century.* New York: Oxford University Press, 1991.

DeBuys, William. *Enchantment and Exploitation: The Life and Hard Times of a New Mexico Mountain Range.* Albuquerque: University of New Mexico Press, 1985.

Elbert, Sarah. "Women and Farming: Changing Structure, Changing Roles." In *Women and Farming: Changing Roles, Changing Structures,* ed. Wava G. Haney and Jane B. Knowles. Boulder, Colo.: Westview Press, 1988.

"Felicia Thal: Cattleman of the Year." *New Mexico Stockman,* November 1993, 82–88.

Flora, Cornelia Butler, and Jan L. Flora. "Structure of Agriculture and Women's Culture in the Great Plains." *Great Plains Quarterly* 8 (Fall 1988): 195–205.

Hartmann, Susan M. *The Home Front and Beyond: American Women in the 1940s.* Boston: Twayne Publishers, 1982.

Hasselstrom, Linda M. *Between Grass and Sky: Where I Live and Work.* Las Vegas: University of Nevada Press, 2002.

———. *Windbreak: A Woman Rancher on the Northern Plains.* Berkeley, Calif.: Barn Owl Books, 1987.

"High-Tech Harvest: Tools Alter How Farmers Do Their Job." *Idaho Statesman,* September 12, 2008, 1, 4, section B.

Hurt, R. Douglas. *Problems of Plenty: The American Farmer in the Twentieth Century.* Chicago: Ivan R. Dee, 2002.

Hussa, Linda. *The Family Ranch: Land, Children, and Tradition in the American West.* Reno: University of Nevada Press, 2009.

"Idaho Dairies Struggle to Hang On." *Idaho Statesman,* April 13, 2010, 1, 4, Section A.

Jellison, Katherine. *Entitled to Power: Farm Women and Technology, 1913–1963.* Chapel Hill: University of North Carolina Press, 1993.

Jensen, Joan. *Calling This Place Home: Women on the Wisconsin Frontier, 1850–1925.* St. Paul: Minnesota Historical Society Press, 2006.

———. "Silver City Health Tourism in the Early Twentieth Century." *New Mexico Historical Review* 84 (Summer 2009): 321–361.

———. *With These Hands: Women Working on the Land.* Old Westbury, N.Y.: Feminist Press, 1981.

Lauters, Amy Mattson. *More Than a Farmer's Wife: Voices of American Farm Women, 1910–1960.* Columbia: University of Missouri Press, 2009.

Lewis, Nancy Owen. "Chasing the Cure in New Mexico: The Lungers and Their Legacy." *El Palacio* 113, no. 4 (Winter 2008): 40–47.

Maret, Elizabeth. *Women of the Range: Women's Roles in the Texas Beef Cattle Industry.* College Station: Texas A&M University Press, 1993.

May, Elaine Tyler. *Homeward Bound: American Families in the Cold War Era.* New York: Basic Books, 1988.

McAndrews, Kristin M. *Wrangling Women: Humor and Gender in the American West.* Reno: University of Nevada Press, 2006.

Moore, David. "Head 'em Out." *New Mexico Magazine,* March 2009, 44–51.

Murphy, Pat. "Flat Top Sheep Ranch: Peavey Country as Far as the Eye Can See." *Idaho Mountain Express,* October 20–26, 1999.

Murphy, Zoe. "Does Your Wife/Husband Help?" *Wallaces' Farmer,* September 20, 1958, 60.

Murray, John. A. *Mythmakers of the West: Shaping America's Imagination.* Flagstaff, Ariz.: Northland Publishing, 2001.

Neel, Susan Rhoades. "Tourism and the American West: New Departures." *Pacific Historical Review* 65 (November 1996): 517–523.

Neth, Mary. *Preserving the Family Farm: Women, Community, and the Foundations of Agribusiness in the Midwest, 1900–1940.* Baltimore: Johns Hopkins University Press, 1995.

Niederman, Sharon. "Three Ranch Women." *Cowboys & Indians* 5 (Spring 1995): 34.

Osterud, Nancy Grey. "Gender and the Transition to Capitalism in Rural America." *Agricultural History* 67 (Spring 1993): 14–29.

Peavey, Diane Josephy. *Bitterbrush Country: Living on the Edge of the Land.* Golden, Colo.: Fulcrum Publishing, 2001.

Pitts, Lee. *Livestock Market Digest,* July 15, 2001.

Pomeroy, Earl. *In Search of the Golden West: The Tourist in Western America.* New York: Alfred A. Knopf, 1957.

Ronayne, Diane. "'Women of Today' Honoree Shares Her Story." *Idaho States-man,* December 6, 2009, C5.

Roosevelt, Theodore. *Ranch Life and the Hunting-Trail.* New York: Century Company, 1899.

Rosenfeld, Rachel. *Farm Women: Work, Farm, and Family in the United States.* Chapel Hill: University of North Carolina Press, 1985.

Rothman, Hal K. "Introduction: Tourism and the Future." In *The Culture of Tourism, the Tourism of Culture: Selling the Past to the Present in the American Southwest.* Albuquerque: University of New Mexico Press, 2003.

———. "Selling the Meaning of Place: Tourism, Entrepreneurship, and Community Transformation in the Twentieth-Century American West." *Pacific Historical Review* 65 (November 1996): 525–557.

Sachs, Caroline. *The Invisible Farmers: Women in Agricultural Production.* Totowa, N.J.: Rowman and Allanheld, 1983.

Sanderson, Rena. "Linda Hasselstrom: The Woman Rancher as Nature Writer." In *Such News of the Land: U.S. Women Nature Writers,* ed. Thomas S. Edwards and Elizabeth A. De Wolfe. Hanover, N.H.: University Press of New England, 2001.

Schackel, Sandra. "Ranch and Farm Women in the Contemporary American West." In *The Rural West since World War II,* ed. R. Douglas Hurt. Lawrence: University Press of Kansas, 1998.

Schwantes, Carlos. *In Mountain Shadows: A History of Idaho.* Lincoln: University of Nebraska Press, 1991.

Seelye, John D. *Memory's Nation: The Place of Plymouth Rock.* Durham: University of North Carolina Press, 1998.

Stoll, Steven. *U.S. Environmentalism since 1945: A Brief History with Documents.* Boston: Bedford/St. Martin's, 2007.

USDA. "Census of Agriculture Shows Growing Diversity in U.S. Farming." February 4, 2009. http://www.usda.gov/wps/portal/usda/usdahome?contentidonly=true&contentid=2009/02/0036.xml.

Van Cleve, Barbara. *Hard Twist: Western Ranch Women.* Santa Fe: Museum of New Mexico Press, 1995.

Weiser Signal American, April 15, 2002.

Woloch, Nancy. *Women and the American Experience,* 4th ed. Boston: McGraw-Hill, 2006.

Wood, Richard E. *Survival of Rural America: Small Victories and Bitter Harvests.* Lawrence: University Press of Kansas, 2008.

Wrobel, David M., and Patrick T. Long, eds. *Seeing and Being Seen: Tourism in the American West.* Lawrence: University Press of Kansas, 2001.

Index